MINIMUM COBOL

CBEMA

Minimum COBOL

PBI

a petrocelli
book

new york / princeton

Printed in the United States of America

1 2 3 4 5 6 7 8 9 10

Library of Congress Cataloging in Publication Data

Computer and Business Equipment Manufacturers Association.
  Minimum COBOL / CBEMA.

  "A Petrocelli book."
  Includes index.
  1. CoBoL (Computer program language) I. Title
QA76.73.C25C68 1977   001.6′424   77–12007
ISBN 0–89433–054–3

CONTENTS

FOREWORD

American National Standard Minimum COBOL is a subset of American National Standard Programming Language COBOL, X3.23–1974. The definition of American National Standard Minimum COBOL was prompted by the need for a COBOL language which provides basic capabilities and yet can exist in environments such as minicomputer and time sharing, which impose resource limitations.

American National Standard Minimum COBOL contains the Nucleus and ten functional processing modules: Table Handling, Sequential I-O, Relative I-O, Indexed I-O, Sort-Merge, Segmentation, Library, Debug, Inter-Program Communication, and Communication. The definition of each of these modules in American National Standard Minimum COBOL is a subset of the full capability of their respective modules in X3.23–1974. The X3.23–1974 module for Report Writer is not included in American National Standard Minimum COBOL.

The Technical Committee X3J4, which developed this standard, has the following personnel:

J. Couperus, Chairman	G. N. Baird, Vice-Chairman	P. A. Beard, Secretary
G. Abrams	M. M. Cook	W. Haccou
G. F. Archer	T. J. Corcoran	C. Hammer
R. M. Barton	J. S. Cousins	C. S. Hansen
R. P. Belmont	M. D. Dent	D. E. Hardy
M. J. Brown	M. P. Gerbauckas	F. Infante
R. C. Bush	K. H. Germann	L. A. Johnson
R. M. Buttler	H. Gordon	J. MacIvor
J. C. Collica	A. T. Greene	B. McKensie

M. Mopper

S. Ng

A. M. Nienhaus

P. Olshansky

W. Osborne

P. Powell

S. S. Root

W. D. Stanford

G. Stephens

M. Topor

D. L. Tucker

M. Vickers

D. Whalen

ACKNOWLEDGMENT

COBOL is an industry language and is not the property of any company or group of companies, or of any organization or group of organizations.

No warranty, expressed or implied, is made by any contributor or by the CODASYL Programming Language Committee as to the accuracy and functioning of the programming system and language. Moreover, no responsibility is assumed by any contributor, or by the committee, in connection therewith.

The authors and copyright holders of the copyrighted material used herein

FLOW-MATIC (trademark of Sperry Rand Corporation), Programming for the UNIVAC (R) I and II, Data Automation Systems copyrighted 1958, 1959, by Sperry Rand Corporation; IBM Commercial Translator Form No. F 28–8013, copyrighted 1959 by IBM; FACT, DSI 27A5260–2760, copyrighted 1960 by Minneapolis-Honeywell

have specifically authorized the use of this material in whole or in part, in the COBOL specifications. Such authorization extends to the reproduction and use of COBOL specifications in programming manuals or similar publications.

SECTION I

Introductory Information

1

INTRODUCTION TO THE STANDARD

1.1 Scope and Purpose

The scope of this standard is to specify both the form and interpretation of programs expressed in American National Standard Minimum COBOL. Its purpose is to define the smallest, useful COBOL capability so that a broader group of users can reap the benefits of a high level business language.

1.2 Structure of Language Specifications

The organization of COBOL specifications in this standard is based on a functional processing module concept. The standard defines a Nucleus and ten functional processing modules: Table Handling, Sequential I-O, Relative I-O, Indexed I-O, Sort-Merge, Segmentation, Library, Debug, Inter-Program Communication, and Communication.

The following is a characterization of the content of each module:

The Nucleus contains language elements that are necessary to perform basic internal operations, i.e., the more elementary options of the various clauses and verbs.

The Table Handling module contains the language elements necessary for: (1) the definition of tables, and (2) reference to the items within tables. This module provides the ability to define fixed length tables of one dimension, and to refer to items within such a table using a subscript.

The Sequential I-O module contains the language elements necessary for the definition and access of sequentially organized external files. The module contains the basic facilities for the definition and access of sequential files.

The Relative I-O module provides the capability of defining and accessing mass storage files in which records are identified by relative record numbers. This module provides basic facilities.

The Indexed I-O module provides the capability of defining mass storage files in which records are identified by the value of a key and accessed through an index. This module provides basic facilities.

The Sort-Merge module provides the capability to order one or more files of records according to a set of user-specified keys contained within each record. Procedures for special handling of each record in the file before and/or after it has been sorted are also provided.

The Segmentation module provides for the overlaying at object time of Procedure Division sections. This module provides for section segment-numbers and fixed segment limits.

The Library module provides the facility for copying COBOL text from a single library into the source program. Text is copied from the library without change.

The Debug module provides a means by which the user can specify optionally compiled debugging lines within the source program.

The Inter-Program Communication (IPC) module provides a facility by which a program can communicate with one or more other programs. This module provides a capability to transfer control to another program known at compile time, and the ability for both programs to have access to certain common data items.

The Communication module provides the ability to access, process and create messages, and to communicate through a Message Control System with local and remote communication devices. The module provides basic facilities to send or receive complete messages.

1.3 Organization of Document

This document is divided into thirteen sections. The first section is composed of the introduction, a summary of elements by module, a list of elements showing their disposition among the various modules, definitions, a discussion of overall language considerations, and a composite language skeleton. Sections II through XII contain specifications for the Nucleus and for each of the ten functional processing modules. These first twelve sections comprise the detailed specifications of American National Standard Minimum COBOL. Section XIII contains the index.

1.4 Definition of an Implementation of American National Standard Minimum COBOL

In terms of the schematic diagram (Table 1) an implementation of American National Standard Minimum COBOL can be represented by a combination of boxes, consisting of one box from each of the eleven vertical columns. Eight modules give the implementation a choice of either all elements within the module or no element within the module. Three modules require the presence of all elements within the module. As illustrations, and for convenience of discourse, the following definitions are provided:

1. A full implementation of American National Standard Minimum COBOL is composed of all elements in the Nucleus and of all elements in each of the ten functional processing modules.

2. A minimum implementation of American National Standard Minimum COBOL is composed of all elements in the Nucleus, Table Handling, and Sequential I-O.

An implementation is defined to meet the requirements of the American National Standard Minimum COBOL specification if that implementation includes all elements in the Nucleus, Table Handling, and Sequential I-O as defined in this standard. It follows from this that, in order to meet the requirements of this standard, any implementation must:

5

Table 1
American National Standard Minimum COBOL

Nucleus	Table Handling	Sequential I-O	Relative I-O	Indexed I-O	Sort-Merge	Segmentation	Library	Debug	Inter-Program Communication	Communication
All elements	All elements	All elements	All elements	All elements	All elements	All elements	All elements	All elements	All elements	All elements
All elements	All elements	All elements	No elements	No elements	No elements	No elements	No elements	No elements	No elements	No elements

1. Not require the inclusion of substitute or additional language elements in the source program, in order to accomplish any part of the function of any of the standard language elements.

2. Accept all standard language elements contained in a module except as specifically exempted in paragraph 1.6.

These points are of particular pertinence in two areas:

1. There are throughout the American National Standard Minimum COBOL specification certain language elements whose syntax or effect is specified to be, in part, implementor-defined. (See paragraph 1.5 for a list of these elements.) While the implementor specifies the constraints on that portion of each element's syntax or rules that is indicated in this standard to be implementor-defined, such constraints may not include any requirement for the inclusion in the source program of substitute or additional language elements.

2. When a function is provided outside the source program that accomplishes a function specified by any particular standard COBOL element, then the implementor must not require, except for Environment Division elements, the specification of that external function in place of or in addition to that standard language element.

The following qualifications apply to the American National Standard Minimum COBOL specifications:

1. There are certain language elements which pertain to specific types of hardware components (see paragraph 1.6 for a list of these elements). In order for an implementation to meet the requirements of this standard, the implementor must specify the minimum hardware configuration required for that implementation and the hardware components that it supports. Further, when support is thus claimed for a specific hardware component, all standard language elements that pertain to that component must be implemented. Language elements that pertain to

specific hardware components for which support is not claimed, need not be implemented. However, the absence of such elements from an implementation of American National Standard Minimum COBOL must be specified.

2. An implementation that includes, in addition to the functional processing modules and the Nucleus, elements or functions that are not defined in the American National Standard Minimum COBOL specifications, meets the requirements of this standard. This is true even though it may imply the extension of the list of reserved words by the implementor, and prevent proper compilation of some programs that meet the requirements of this standard. The implementor must specify any extensions (language elements or functions not defined in this standard) that are included in the implementation. The implementor must also specify the language elements implemented which are included in a module when that complete module is not implemented.

3. In general, the American National Standard Minimum COBOL specification specifies no upper limit on such things as the number of statements in a program, the number of operands permitted in certain statements, etc. It is recognized that these limits will vary from one implementation of American National Standard Minimum COBOL to another and may prevent the proper compilation of some programs that meet the requirements of this standard.

4. For a discussion of character substitution which likewise may prevent the proper compilation of some programs that meet the requirements of this standard, see paragraph 4.3.1, Character Set.

1.5 Implementor-Defined Language Specifications

The language elements in the following lists depend on implementor definitions to complete the specification of the syntax or rules for the elements.

The elements whose syntax is partly implementor-defined are:

Element	Implementor-Defined Aspect
SOURCE-COMPUTER paragraph	Computer-name
OBJECT-COMPUTER paragraph	Computer-name
ASSIGN clause	Implementor-name
VALUE OF clause	Implementor-name; whether implementor-names are provided
CALL statement	Relationship between operand and the referenced program
COPY statement	Relationship between text-name and the library
Margin R	The location
Area B	The number of character positions

The elements whose effect is partly implementor-defined are:

Element	Implementor-Defined Aspect
USAGE IS COMPUTATIONAL clause	Representation and whether automatic alignment occurs
SYNCHRONIZED clause	Whether implicit FILLER positions are generated; their effect on the size of the group items and redefining items
ACCEPT statement	Maximum size of one transfer of data
DISPLAY statement	Maximum size of one transfer of data
Numeric test	Representation of valid sign

1.6 Elements that Pertain to Specific Hardware Components

The standard language elements in the list that follows pertains to specific types of hardware components. These language elements must be implemented in any implementation of American National Standard Minimum COBOL when support is claimed, by the implementor, for the specific types of hardware components to which they pertain, and the module in which they are defined is included in that implementation.

Element	*Hardware Component*
OPEN . . . I-O statement (Sequential I-O only)	Mass storage
REWRITE statement (Sequential I-O only)	Mass storage
SEND . . . BEFORE/AFTER ADVANCING statement	Devices capable of vertical positioning
WRITE . . . BEFORE/AFTER ADVANCING	Devices capable of vertical positioning
All elements of Relative I-O module	Mass storage
All elements of Indexed I-O module	Mass storage

2

SUMMARY OF ELEMENTS BY MODULE

2.1 General Description

This chapter contains a summary of all elements in the American National Standard Minimum COBOL organized according to the Nucleus and the functional processing modules. For information purposes the summary also includes all elements in the same modules within American National Standard COBOL X3.23–1974.

The column titled "ANSI Minimum" specifies the elements of American National Standard Minimum COBOL. The column titled "ANSI Level 1" specifies the level 1 elements of American National Standard COBOL X3.23–1974. The column titled "ANSI Level 2" specifies the level 2 elements of American National Standard COBOL X3.23–1974.

The letter S in a column indicates the presence of the specified element. The letter N in a column indicates the absence of the specified element.

Below is a list of the summary of elements by module shown on the following pages:

Summary of elements in the Nucleus

Summary of elements in the Table Handling module

Summary of elements in the Sequential I-O module

Summary of elements in the Relative I-O module

Summary of elements in the Indexed I-O module

Summary of elements in the Sort-Merge module

Summary of elements in the Segmentation module

Summary of elements in the Library module

Summary of elements in the Debug module

Summary of elements in the Inter-Program Communication module

Summary of elements in the Communication module

Summary of Elements in the Nucleus

Elements	ANSI Minimum	ANSI Level 1	ANSI Level 2
Language Concepts			
Character set			
Characters used in words 0-9 A-Z - (hyphen)	X	X	X
Characters used in punctuation " ( ) . space	X	X	X
comma semicolon	X	N	X
Characters used in editing B + −., Z * $	X	X	X
O CR DB /	N	X	X
Characters used in arithmetic operations + − * / **	N	N	X
Characters used in relation conditions > < = ...	X	N	X
Separators			
The separators, semicolon and comma, are allowed	X	N	X
Character-strings			
COBOL words			
Maximum of 15 characters . .	X	N	N
Maximum of 30 characters . .	N	X	X
User-defined words			
Data-name must begin with an alphabetic character	X	X	N
Data-name need not begin with an alphabetic character . . .	N	N	X
Data-name must be unique; may not be qualified	X	X	N
Data-name may be qualified .	N	N	X
Level-number	X	X	X

Summary of Elements in the Nucleus (cont.)

Elements	ANSI Minimum	ANSI Level 1	ANSI Level 2
Mnemonic-name	N	X	X
Paragraph-name	X	X	X
Program-name	X	X	X
Routine-name	N	X	X
Section-name	X	X	X
Condition-name	N	N	X
System-name			
Computer-name	X	X	X
Implementor-name	X	X	X
Language-name	N	X	X
Reserved words			
Key words	X	X	X
Optional words	X	X	X
Figurative constants: ZERO, SPACE	X	X	X
Figurative constants: ZEROS, ZEROES, SPACES	X	N	X
Figurative constants: HIGH-VALUE, LOW-VALUE, QUOTE	N	X	X
Figurative constants: HIGH-VALUES, LOW-VALUES, QUOTES, ALL literal . . .	N	N	X
Special-character words > < =	X	N	X
Connectives			
Qualifier connectives: OF, IN	N	N	X
Series connectives: , (separator comma) and ; (separator semicolon)	X	N	X
Logical connectives: AND, OR, AND NOT, OR NOT	N	N	X
Literals			
Numeric literals: 1 to 18 digits .	X	X	X
Nonnumeric literals: 1 to 120 characters	X	X	X
PICTURE character-strings . . .	X	X	X
Comment-entries	N	X	X

Summary of Elements in the Nucleus (cont.)

Elements	ANSI Minimum	ANSI Level 1	ANSI Level 2
Qualification			
No qualification permitted; unique names only	X	X	N
Qualification permitted	N	N	X
Reference format			
Sequence number	X	X	X
Continuation of lines:			
Continuation of nonnumeric literals	X	X	X
Continuation of words and numeric literals	N	N	X
Comment lines			
Asterisk (*) comment line . .	X	X	X
Stroke (/) comment line . . .	X	X	X
Identification Division			
PROGRAM-ID paragraph	X	X	X
AUTHOR paragraph	N	X	X
INSTALLATION paragraph . .	N	X	X
DATE-WRITTEN paragraph . .	N	X	X
DATE-COMPILED paragraph .	N	N	X
SECURITY paragraph	N	X	X
Environment Division			
Configuration Section			
SOURCE-COMPUTER paragraph	X	X	X
OBJECT-COMPUTER paragraph			
Computer-name	X	X	X
MEMORY SIZE clause . . .	N	X	X
PROGRAM COLLATING SE-QUENCE clause	N	X	X
SPECIAL-NAMES paragraph			
Alphabet-name clause	N	X	X
STANDARD-1 option . . .	N	X	X
NATIVE option	N	X	X
Implementor-name option . .	N	X	X
Literal option	N	N	X

Summary of Elements in the Nucleus (cont.)

Elements	ANSI Minimum	ANSI Level 1	ANSI Level 2
CURRENCY SIGN clause . .	X	X	X
DECIMAL-POINT clause . .	X	X	X
Implementor-name IS mnemonic-name	N	X	X
ON STATUS	N	X	X
OFF STATUS	N	X	X
Implementor-name series . . .	N	X	X

Data Division

Working-Storage Section

Record description entry	X	X	X
Data description entry	X	X	X
BLANK WHEN ZERO clause .	N	X	X
Data-name or FILLER clause . .	X	X	X
JUSTIFIED clause (or JUST clause)	N	X	X
Level-number			
01 through 10	X	X	N
01 through 49	N	N	X
Must be two digits	X	X	N
May be one or two digits . . .	N	N	X
66	N	N	X
77	N	X	X
88	N	N	X
PICTURE clause (or PIC clause) .	X	X	X
Character-string may contain 30 characters	X	X	X
Data characters: X 9	X	X	X
Data character: A	N	X	X
Operational symbols: S V . . .	X	X	X
Operational symbol: P	N	X	X
Fixed insertion characters B + − . , $	X	X	X
Fixed insertion characters O CR DB /	N	X	X
Replacement or floating characters $ + − Z *	X	X	X

15

Summary of Elements in the Nucleus (cont.)

Elements	ANSI Minimum	ANSI Level 1	ANSI Level 2
Currency sign substitution . .	X	X	X
Decimal point substitution . .	X	X	X
REDEFINES clause:			
May not be nested	X	X	N
May be nested	N	N	X
RENAMES clause	N	N	X
SIGN clause	X	X	X
SYNCHRONIZED clause (or SYNC clause)	X	X	X
USAGE clause	X	X	X
DISPLAY	X	X	X
COMPUTATIONAL (or COMP)	X	X	X
VALUE clause	X	X	X
Literal	X	X	X
Literal series	N	N	X
Literal-1 THRU literal-2 . . .	N	N	X
Literal range series	N	N	X

Procedure Division

Elements	ANSI Minimum	ANSI Level 1	ANSI Level 2
Arithmetic Expressions	N	N	X
Conditional expressions			
Simple condition	X	X	X
Relation condition	X	X	X
Relational operators			
[NOT] GREATER THAN	X	X	X
[NOT] >	X	N	X
[NOT] LESS THAN . . .	X	X	X
[NOT] <	X	N	X
[NOT] EQUAL TO . . .	X	X	X
[NOT] = ...	X	N	X
Comparison of numeric operands	X	X	X
Comparison of nonnumeric operands			
Operands must be of equal size	N	X	N
Operands of unequal size are permitted	X	N	X

Summary of Elements in the Nucleus (cont.)

Elements	ANSI Minimum	ANSI Level 1	ANSI Level 2
Class condition	X	X	X
Condition-name condition . .	N	N	X
Sign condition	N	N	X
Switch-status condition . . .	N	X	X
Complex condition			
Logical operators AND, OR, NOT	N	N	X
Negated simple condition . . .	N	N	X
Combined condition			
Simple conditions and negated simple conditions may be combined	N	N	X
Parenthesized conditions . .	N	N	X
Abbreviated combined relation condition	N	N	X
Arithmetic statements			
Arithmetic operands limited to 18 digits	X	X	X
ACCEPT statement	X	X	X
Only one transfer of data . . .	X	X	N
No restrictions on the number of transfers of data	N	N	X
FROM mnemonic-name phrase .	N	N	X
FROM DATE/DAY/TIME phrase	N	N	X
ADD statement	X	X	X
Identifier/literal series	N	X	X
TO identifier	X	X	X
TO identifier series	N	N	X
GIVING identifier	X	X	X
GIVING identifier series . . .	N	N	X
ROUNDED phrase	X	X	X
SIZE ERROR phrase	N	X	X
CORRESPONDING phrase . .	N	N	X
ALTER statement	N	X	X
Only one procedure-name . . .	N	X	N
Procedure-name series . . .	N	N	X

17

Summary of Elements in the Nucleus (cont.)

Elements	*ANSI* *Minimum*	*ANSI* *Level 1*	*ANSI* *Level 2*
COMPUTE statement	N	N	X
Arithmetic expression	N	N	X
Identifier series	N	N	X
ROUNDED phrase	N	N	X
SIZE ERROR phrase	N	N	X
DISPLAY statement	X	X	X
Only one transfer of data . . .	X	X	N
No restrictions on the number of transfers of data	N	N	X
Identifier/literal	X	X	X
Identifier/literal series	N	X	X
UPON mnemonic-name phrase .	N	N	X
DIVIDE statement	X	X	X
INTO identifier	N	X	X
INTO identifier series	N	N	X
BY identifier/literal	X	X	X
GIVING identifier	X	X	X
GIVING identifier series	N	N	X
REMAINDER phrase	N	N	X
ROUNDED phrase	X	X	X
SIZE ERROR phrase	N	X	X
ENTER statement	N	X	X
EXIT statement	N	X	X
GO TO statement	X	X	X
Procedure-name is required . .	X	X	N
Procedure-name may be omitted .	N	N	X
DEPENDING ON phrase . . .	X	X	X
IF statement	X	X	X
Limited to one or more imperative verbs	X	X	N
Not limited to imperative verbs .	N	N	X
Nested statements	N	N	X
ELSE phrase	X	X	X
NEXT SENTENCE phrase . . .	N	X	X
INSPECT statement	N	X	X
Only single character data item .	N	X	N
Multi-character data items . . .	N	N	X

18

Summary of Elements in the Nucleus (cont.)

Elements	ANSI Minimum	ANSI Level 1	ANSI Level 2
TALLYING phrase	N	X	X
BEFORE/AFTER INITIAL option	N	X	X
REPLACING phrase	N	X	X
TALLYING and REPLACING phrases	N	X	X
Series	N	N	X
MOVE statement	X	X	X
TO identifier	X	X	X
Identifier series	N	X	X
CORRESPONDING phrase . .	N	N	X
MULTIPLY statement	X	X	X
BY identifier	X	X	X
BY identifier series	N	N	X
GIVING identifier	X	X	X
GIVING identifier series	N	N	X
ROUNDED phrase	X	X	X
SIZE ERROR phrase	N	X	X
PERFORM statement	X	X	X
Procedure-name	X	X	X
THRU phrase	X	X	X
TIMES phrase	X	X	X
UNTIL phrase	X	N	X
VARYING phrase	N	N	X
STOP statement	X	X	X
Literal	N	X	X
RUN	X	X	X
STRING statement	N	N	X
DELIMITED series	N	N	X
POINTER phrase	N	N	X
ON OVERFLOW phrase . . .	N	N	X
SUBTRACT statement	X	X	X
Identifier/literal series	N	X	X
FROM identifier	X	X	X
FROM identifier series	N	N	X
GIVING identifier	X	X	X
GIVING identifier series	N	N	X
ROUNDED phrase	X	X	X

Summary of Elements in the Nucleus (cont.)

Elements	ANSI Minimum	ANSI Level 1	ANSI Level 2
SIZE ERROR phrase	N	X	X
CORRESPONDING phrase . .	N	N	X
UNSTRING statement	N	N	X
DELIMITED BY phrase . . .	N	N	X
POINTER phrase	N	N	X
TALLYING phrase	N	N	X
ON OVERFLOW phrase . . .	N	N	X

Summary of Elements in the Table Handling Module

Elements	ANSI Minimum	ANSI Level 1	ANSI Level 2
LANGUAGE Concepts			
User-defined words			
Index-name	N	X	X
Subscripting			
1 level only	X	N	N
1, 2, or 3 levels permitted . . .	N	X	X
Indexing			
1, 2, or 3 levels permitted . . .	N	X	X
Data Division			
OCCURS clause	X	X	X
Integer TIMES	X	X	X
Integer-1 TO integer-2 DEPEND-ING on data-name	N	N	X
ASCENDING/DESCENDING data-name	N	N	X
ASCENDING/DESCENDING data-name series	N	N	X
ASCENDING/DESCENDING series	N	N	X
INDEXED BY index-name phrase	N	X	X
INDEXED BY index-name phrase series	N	X	X
USAGE IS INDEX clause	N	X	X

20

Summary of Elements in the Table Handling Module (cont.)

Elements	ANSI Minimum	ANSI Level 1	ANSI Level 2
Procedure Division			
SEARCH statement	N	N	X
VARYING phrase	N	N	X
AT END phrase	N	N	X
WHEN phrase	N	N	X
WHEN phrase series	N	N	X
SEARCH ALL statement	N	N	X
AT END phrase	N	N	X
WHEN phrase	N	N	X
SET statement	N	X	X
Index-name/identifier	N	X	X
Index-name/identifier series . . .	N	X	X
UP BY identifier/integer	N	X	X
DOWN BY identifier/integer . .	N	X	X
Index-name series	N	X	X

Summary of Elements in the Sequential I-O Module

Elements	ANSI Minimum	ANSI Level 1	ANSI Level 2
Language Concepts			
User-defined words			
File-name	X	X	X
Record-name	X	X	X
I-O status	X	X	X
Special register			
LINAGE-COUNTER	N	N	X
Environment Division			
Input-Output Section			
FILE-CONTROL paragraph . .	X	X	X
File control entry	X	X	X
SELECT clause	X	X	X
OPTIONAL phrase	N	N	X
ASSIGN clause	X	X	X

Summary of Elements in the Sequential I-O Module (cont.)

Elements	ANSI Minimum	ANSI Level 1	ANSI Level 2
ORGANIZATION IS SEQUENTIAL clause	X	X	X
ACCESS MODE IS SEQUENTIAL clause	X	X	X
FILE STATUS clause	X	X	X
RESERVE integer AREA(S) clause	N	N	X
I-O-CONTROL paragraph	N	X	X
RERUN clause	N	X	X
SAME AREA clause	N	X	X
SAME AREA series	N	X	X
SAME RECORD AREA clause	N	N	X
SAME RECORD AREA series	N	N	X
MULTIPLE FILE TAPE clause	N	N	X

Data Division

File Section

Elements	ANSI Minimum	ANSI Level 1	ANSI Level 2
File description entry	X	X	X
Record description entry	X	X	X
BLOCK CONTAINS clause	X	X	X
Integer RECORDS/CHARACTERS	X	X	X
Integer-1 TO integer-2 RECORDS/CHARACTERS	N	N	X
CODE-SET clause	N	X	X
DATA RECORDS clause	N	X	X
Data-name	N	X	X
Data-name series	N	X	X
LABEL RECORDS clause	X	X	X
STANDARD	X	X	X
OMITTED	X	X	X
LINAGE clause	N	N	X
FOOTING phrase	N	N	X
TOP phrase	N	N	X
BOTTOM phrase	N	N	X

Summary of Elements in the Sequential I-O Module (cont.)

Elements	ANSI Minimum	ANSI Level 1	ANSI Level 2
RECORD CONTAINS clause . .	N	X	X
Integer-1 TO integer-2 CHARAC-TERS	N	X	X
VALUE OF clause	X	X	X
Implementor-name IS literal . .	X	X	X
Implementor-name IS literal series	N	X	X
Implementor-name IS data-name	N	N	X
Implementor-name IS data-name series	N	N	X
Procedure Division			
CLOSE statement	X	X	X
Single file-name	X	X	X
File-name series	N	N	X
REEL/UNIT	N	X	X
WITH LOCK phrase	N	N	X
WITH NO REWIND phrase . .	N	N	X
FOR REMOVAL phrase . . .	N	N	X
OPEN statement	X	X	X
Single file-name	X	X	X
File-name series	N	N	X
INPUT phrase	X	X	X
REVERSED phrase	N	N	X
WITH NO REWIND phrase .	N	N	X
OUTPUT phrase	X	X	X
NO REWIND phrase	N	N	X
I-O phrase	X	X	X
EXTEND phrase	N	N	X
INPUT, OUTPUT, I-O, and EX-TEND series	N	N	X
READ statement	X	X	X
INTO identifier	N	X	X
AT END phrase required . . .	X	N	N
AT END phrase optional . . .	N	X	X
REWRITE statement	X	X	X
FROM identifier	N	X	X

Summary of Elements in the Sequential I-O Module (cont.)

Elements	ANSI Minimum	ANSI Level 1	ANSI Level 2
USE statement	N	X	X
EXCEPTION/ERROR PROCE-			
DURE phrase	N	X	X
ON file-name	N	X	X
ON INPUT	N	X	X
ON OUTPUT	N	X	X
ON I-O	N	X	X
ON EXTEND	N	N	X
ON file-name series	N	N	X
WRITE statement	X	X	X
FROM identifier	N	X	X
BEFORE/AFTER ADVANCING			
phrase	X	X	X
integer	X	X	X
integer LINE/LINES	N	X	X
identifier	X	X	X
identifier LINE/LINES . . .	N	X	X
mnemonic-name	N	N	X
PAGE	X	X	X
AT END-OF-PAGE phrase . .	N	N	X

Summary of Elements in the Relative I-O Module

Elements	ANSI Minimum	ANSI Level 1	ANSI Level 2
Language Concepts			
User-defined words			
File-name	X	X	X
Record-name	X	X	X
I-O status	X	X	X
Environment Division			
Input-Output Section			
FILE-CONTROL paragraph . .	X	X	X
File control entry	X	X	X
SELECT clause	X	X	X
ASSIGN clause	X	X	X

Summary of Elements in the Relative I-O Module (cont.)

Elements	ANSI Minimum	ANSI Level 1	ANSI Level 2
ORGANIZATION IS RELATIVE clause	X	X	X
ACCESS MODE clause . . .	X	X	X
SEQUENTIAL	X	X	X
RELATIVE KEY phrase .	X	X	X
RANDOM	X	X	X
RELATIVE KEY phrase .	X	X	X
DYNAMIC	N	N	X
RELATIVE KEY phrase .	N	N	X
FILE STATUS clause	X	X	X
RESERVE integer AREA(S) clause	N	N	X
I-O-CONTROL paragraph . . .	N	X	X
RERUN clause	N	X	X
SAME AREA clause	N	X	X
SAME AREA series	N	X	X
SAME RECORD AREA clause	N	N	X
SAME RECORD AREA series	N	N	X

Data Division

File Section

Elements	ANSI Minimum	ANSI Level 1	ANSI Level 2
File description entry	X	X	X
Record description entry	X	X	X
BLOCK CONTAINS clause . .	X	X	X
Integer RECORDS/CHARACTERS	X	X	X
Integer-1 TO integer-2 RECORDS/CHARACTERS . . .	N	N	X
DATA RECORDS clause . . .	N	X	X
Data-name	N	X	X
Data-name series	N	X	X
LABEL RECORDS clause . . .	X	X	X
STANDARD	X	X	X
OMITTED	X	X	X
RECORD CONTAINS clause . .	N	X	X
Integer-1 TO integer-2 CHARACTERS	N	X	X

Summary of Elements in the Relative I-O Module (cont.)

Elements	ANSI Minimum	ANSI Level 1	ANSI Level 2
VALUE OF clause	X	X	X
Implementor-name IS literal . .	X	X	X
Implementor-name IS literal series	N	X	X
Implementor-name IS data-name	N	N	X
Implementor-name IS data-name series	N	N	X

Procedure Division

Elements	ANSI Minimum	ANSI Level 1	ANSI Level 2
CLOSE statement	X	X	X
Single file-name	X	X	X
File-name series	N	X	X
WITH LOCK phrase	N	X	X
DELETE statement	X	X	X
INVALID KEY phrase	X	X	X
OPEN statement	X	X	X
Single file-name	X	X	X
File-name series	N	X	X
INPUT phrase	X	X	X
OUTPUT phrase	X	X	X
I-O phrase	X	X	X
INPUT, OUTPUT, and I-O series	N	X	X
READ statement	X	X	X
INTO identifier	N	X	X
NEXT phrase	N	N	X
AT END phrase required . . .	X	N	N
AT END phrase optional . . .	N	X	X
INVALID KEY phrase required .	X	N	N
INVALID KEY phrase optional .	N	X	X
REWRITE statement	X	X	X
FROM identifier	N	X	X
INVALID KEY phrase	X	X	X
START statement	N	N	X
KEY IS phrase	N	N	X
INVALID KEY phrase	N	N	X
USE statement	N	X	X

Summary of Elements in the Relative I-O Module (cont.)

Elements	ANSI Minimum	ANSI Level 1	ANSI Level 2
EXCEPTION/ERROR PROCE-DURE phrase	N	X	X
ON file-name	N	X	X
ON INPUT	N	X	X
ON OUTPUT	N	X	X
ON I-O	N	X	X
ON file-name series	N	N	X
WRITE statement	X	X	X
FROM identifier	N	X	X
INVALID KEY phrase required	X	N	N
INVALID KEY phrase optional	N	X	X

Summary of Elements in the Indexed I-O Module

Elements	ANSI Minimum	ANSI Level 1	ANSI Level 2
Language Concepts			
User-defined words			
File-name	X	X	X
Record-name	X	X	X
I-O status	X	X	X
Environment Division			
Input-Output Section			
FILE-CONTROL paragraph	X	X	X
File control entry	X	X	X
SELECT clause	X	X	X
ASSIGN clause	X	X	X
ORGANIZATION IS INDEXED clause	X	X	X
ACCESS MODE clause	X	X	X
SEQUENTIAL	X	X	X
RANDOM	X	X	X
DYNAMIC	N	N	X
RECORD KEY clause	X	X	X

27

Summary of Elements in the Indexed I-O Module (cont.)

Elements	ANSI Minimum	ANSI Level 1	ANSI Level 2
ALTERNATE RECORD KEY clause	N	N	X
WITH DUPLICATES phrase .	N	N	X
FILE STATUS clause	X	X	X
RESERVE integer AREA(S) clause	N	N	X
I-O-CONTROL paragraph . . .	N	X	X
RERUN clause	N	X	X
SAME AREA clause	N	X	X
SAME AREA series	N	X	X
SAME RECORD AREA clause	N	N	X
SAME RECORD AREA series	N	N	X

Data Division

File Section

File description entry	X	X	X
Record description entry	X	X	X
BLOCK CONTAINS clause . .	X	X	X
Integer RECORDS/CHARAC-TERS	X	X	X
Integer-1 TO integer-2 RE-CORDS/CHARACTERS . .	N	N	X
DATA RECORDS clause . . .	N	X	X
Data-name	N	X	X
Data-name series	N	X	X
LABEL RECORDS clause . . .	X	X	X
STANDARD	X	X	X
OMITTED	X	X	X
RECORD CONTAINS clause . .	N	X	X
Integer-1 TO integer-2 CHARAC-TERS	N	X	X
VALUE OF clause	X	X	X
Implementor-name IS literal . .	X	X	X
Implementor-name IS literal series	N	X	X
Implementor-name IS data-name	N	N	X
Implementor-name IS data-name series	N	N	X

Summary of Elements in the Indexed I-O Module (cont.)

Elements	ANSI Minimum	ANSI Level 1	ANSI Level 2
Procedure Division			
CLOSE statement	X	X	X
Single file-name	X	X	X
File-name series	N	X	X
WITH LOCK phrase	N	X	X
DELETE statement	X	X	X
INVALID KEY phrase	X	X	X
OPEN statement	X	X	X
Single file-name	X	X	X
File-name series	N	X	X
INPUT phrase	X	X	X
OUTPUT phrase	X	X	X
I-O phrase	X	X	X
INPUT, OUTPUT, and I-O series	N	X	X
READ statement	X	X	X
INTO identifier	N	X	X
KEY IS phrase	N	N	X
NEXT phrase	N	N	X
AT END phrase required . . .	X	N	N
AT END phrase optional . . .	N	X	X
INVALID KEY phrase required .	X	N	N
INVALID KEY phrase optional .	N	X	X
REWRITE statement	X	X	X
FROM identifier	N	X	X
INVALID KEY phrase required .	X	N	N
INVALID KEY phrase optional .	N	X	X
START statement	N	N	X
KEY IS phrase	N	N	X
INVALID KEY phrase	N	N	X
USE statement	N	X	X
EXCEPTION/ERROR PROCE-DURE phrase	N	X	X
ON file-name	N	X	X
ON INPUT	N	X	X
ON OUTPUT	N	X	X
ON I-O	N	X	X
ON file-name series	N	N	X

Summary of Elements in the Indexed I-O Module (cont.)

Elements	ANSI Minimum	ANSI Level 1	ANSI Level 2
WRITE statement	X	X	X
FROM identifier	N	X	X
INVALID KEY phrase required .	X	N	N
INVALID KEY phrase optional .	N	X	X

Summary of Elements in the Sort-Merge Module

Elements	ANSI Minimum	ANSI Level 1	ANSI Level 2
Language Concepts			
User-defined words			
File-name	X	X	X
Environment Division			
Input-Output Section			
FILE-CONTROL paragraph . .	X	X	X
File control entry	X	X	X
SELECT clause	X	X	X
ASSIGN clause	X	X	X
I-O-CONTROL paragraph . . .	N	N	X
SAME RECORD AREA clause	N	N	X
SAME RECORD AREA series	N	N	X
SAME SORT/SORT-MERGE AREA clause	N	N	X
SAME SORT/SORT-MERGE AREA series	N	N	X
Data Division			
File Section			
Sort-merge file description entry .	X	X	X
DATA RECORDS clause . . .	N	X	X
Data-name	N	X	X
Data-name series	N	X	X
RECORD CONTAINS clause . .	N	X	X
Integer-1 TO integer-2 CHARACTERS	N	X	X

Summary of Elements in the Sort-Merge Module (cont.)

Elements	ANSI Minimum	ANSI Level 1	ANSI Level 2
Procedure Division			
MERGE statement	N	N	X
KEY data-name	N	N	X
KEY data-name series	N	N	X
ASCENDING series	N	N	X
DESCENDING series	N	N	X
Mixed ASCENDING/DESCENDING	N	N	X
COLLATING SEQUENCE phrase	N	N	X
USING phrase	N	N	X
OUTPUT PROCEDURE phrase .	N	N	X
GIVING phrase	N	N	X
RELEASE statement	X	X	X
FROM phrase	N	X	X
RETURN statement	X	X	X
INTO phrase	N	X	X
AT END phrase	X	X	X
SORT statement	X	X	X
Only one SORT statement per program	N	X	N
Multiple SORT statements per program	X	N	X
KEY data-name	X	X	X
KEY data-name series	X	X	X
ASCENDING series	X	X	X
DESCENDING series	X	X	X
Mixed ASCENDING/DESCENDING	X	X	X
COLLATING SEQUENCE phrase	N	N	X
INPUT PROCEDURE phrase . .	X	X	X
USING phrase	X	X	X
OUTPUT PROCEDURE phrase .	X	X	X
GIVING phrase	X	X	X

31

Summary of Elements in the Segmentation Module

Elements	ANSI Minimum	ANSI Level 1	ANSI Level 2
Language Concepts			
User-defined words			
Segment-number	X	X	X
Environment Division			
OBJECT-COMPUTER paragraph			
SEGMENT-LIMIT clause . . .	N	N	X
Procedure Division			
Segment-numbers 0 through 49 for permanent segments	X	X	X
Segment-numbers 50 through 99 for independent segments	X	X	X
All sections with the same segment-number must be together in the source program	X	X	N
Sections with the same segment-number need not be physically contiguous in the source program	N	N	X

Summary of Elements in the Library Module

Elements	ANSI Minimum	ANSI Level 1	ANSI Level 2
Language Concepts			
User-defined words			
Text-name	X	X	X
Library-name	N	N	X
All Divisions			
COPY statement	X	X	X
OF library-name phrase	N	N	X
REPLACING phrase	N	N	X

Summary of Elements in the Debug Module

Elements	ANSI Minimum	ANSI Level 1	ANSI Level 2
Language Concepts			
Special registers			
DEBUG-ITEM	N	X	X
Environment Division			
SOURCE-COMPUTER paragraph			
WITH DEBUGGING MODE clause	X	X	X
Procedure Division			
USE FOR DEBUGGING statement	N	X	X
Procedure-name	N	X	X
Procedure-name series	N	X	X
ALL PROCEDURES	N	X	X
ALL REFERENCES OF identifier series	N	N	X
File-name series	N	N	X
Cd-name series	N	N	X
All Divisions			
Debugging lines	X	X	X

Summary of Elements in the Inter-Program Communication Module

Elements	ANSI Minimum	ANSI Level 1	ANSI Level 2
Data Division			
Linkage Section	X	X	X
Procedure Division			
Procedure Division header			
USING phrase	X	X	X
At least five data-names permitted	X	N	N

Summary of Elements in the Inter-Program Communication Module (cont.)

Elements	ANSI Minimum	ANSI Level 1	ANSI Level 2
CALL statement	X	X	X
Literal	X	X	X
Identifier	N	N	X
USING phrase	X	X	X
At least five data-names permitted	X	N	N
ON OVERFLOW phrase . . .	N	N	X
CANCEL statement	N	N	X
EXIT PROGRAM statement . . .	X	X	X

Summary of Elements in the Communication Module

Elements	ANSI Minimum	ANSI Level 1	ANSI Level 2
Language Concepts			
User-defined words			
Cd-name	X	X	X
Data Division			
Communication Section			
Communication description entry .	X	X	X
FOR INPUT clause	X	X	X
INITIAL phrase	N	N	X
END KEY clause	X	X	X
MESSAGE COUNT clause .	X	X	X
MESSAGE DATE clause . .	X	X	X
MESSAGE TIME clause . .	X	X	X
SYMBOLIC QUEUE clause .	X	X	X
SYMBOLIC SOURCE clause	X	X	X
SYMBOLIC SUB-QUEUE-n clause	N	X	X
STATUS KEY clause . . .	X	X	X
TEXT LENGTH clause . .	X	X	X

Summary of Elements in the Communication Module (cont.)

Elements	ANSI Minimum	ANSI Level 1	ANSI Level 2
FOR OUTPUT clause	X	X	X
DESTINATION COUNT clause	X	X	X
DESTINATION TABLE clause	N	X	X
INDEXED BY phrase . .	N	X	X
ERROR KEY clause . . .	X	X	X
SYMBOLIC DESTINATION clause	X	X	X
STATUS KEY clause . . .	X	X	X
TEXT LENGTH clause . .	X	X	X

Procedure Division

Elements	ANSI Minimum	ANSI Level 1	ANSI Level 2
ACCEPT MESSAGE COUNT statement	X	X	X
DISABLE statement	N	X	X
INPUT phrase	N	X	X
TERMINAL phrase	N	N	X
OUTPUT phrase	N	X	X
KEY identifier/literal phrase . .	N	X	X
ENABLE statement	N	X	X
INPUT phrase	N	X	X
TERMINAL phrase	N	N	X
OUTPUT phrase	N	X	X
KEY identifier/literal phrase . .	N	X	X
RECEIVE statement	X	X	X
MESSAGE phrase	X	X	X
SEGMENT phrase	N	N	X
INTO identifier phrase	X	X	X
NO DATA phrase	X	X	X
SEND statement	X	X	X
FROM identifier phrase	X	X	X
WITH EMI phrase	X	X	X
WITH EGI phrase	X	X	X
WITH ESI phrase	N	N	X
WITH identifier phrase	N	N	X

35

Summary of Elements in the Communication Module (cont.)

Elements	ANSI Minimum	ANSI Level 1	ANSI Level 2
BEFORE/AFTER ADVANCING phrase	X	X	X
integer	X	X	X
integer LINE/LINES	N	X	X
identifier	X	X	X
identifier LINE/LINES	N	X	X
mnemonic-name	N	X	X
PAGE	X	X	X

3

LIST OF ELEMENTS SHOWING DISPOSITION

3.1 General Discription

This chapter contains a list of all elements in American National Standard Minimum COBOL showing the module in which each element is introduced.

Elements	*Module*
Language Concepts	
Character set	
Characters used for words C-9 A-Z - (hyphen)	Nucleus
Characters used for puncutation " ( ) . space	Nucleus
comma semicolon	Nucleus
Characters used in editing B + −. , Z * $	Nucleus
Characters used in relation condition > < =	Nucleus
Separators	Nucleus
The separators, semicolon and comma, are allowed	Nucleus
Character-strings	Nucleus
COBOL words	Nucleus
Maximum of 15 characters	Nucleus
User-defined words	Nucleus
Cd-name	Communication
Data-name must begin with an alphabetic character	Nucleus
Data-name must be unique; may not be qualified	Nucleus

Elements	*Module*
File-name	Sequential I-O
. . . .	Relative I-O
. . . .	Indexed I-O
. . . .	Sort-Merge
Index-name	Table Handling
Level-number	Nucleus
Paragraph-name	Nucleus
Program-name	Nucleus
Record-name	Sequential I-O
. . . .	Relative I-O
. . . .	Indexed I-O
Section-name	Nucleus
Segment-number	Segmentation
Text-name	Library
System-name	Nucleus
Computer-name	Nucleus
Implementor-name	Sequential I-O
. . . .	Relative I-O
. . . .	Indexed I-O
. . . .	Sort-Merge
Reserved words	Nucleus
Key words	Nucleus
Optional words	Nucleus
Figurative constants: ZERO, ZEROS, ZEROES, SPACE, SPACES . . .	Nucleus
Special-character words $>$ $<$ $=$ . . .	Nucleus
Series connectives: , (separator comma) and ; (separator semicolon)	Nucleus
Literals	
Numeric literals: 1 to 18 digits . . .	Nucleus
Nonnumeric literals: 1 to 120 characters	Nucleus
PICTURE character-strings	Nucleus
Qualification	
No qualification permitted; unique names only	Nucleus

Elements	*Module*
Subscripting	
1 level only	Table Handling
Reference format	
Sequence number	Nucleus
Continuation of nonnumeric literals	Nucleus
Comment lines	Nucleus
Asterisk (*) comment line	Nucleus
Stroke (/) comment line	Nucleus
Identification Division	
PROGRAM-ID paragraph	Nucleus
Environment Division	
Configuration Section	
SOURCE-COMPUTER paragraph . . .	Nucleus
Computer-name	Nucleus
WITH DEBUGGING MODE clause	Debug
OBJECT-COMPUTER paragraph . . .	Nucleus
Computer-name	Nucleus
SPECIAL-NAMES paragraph	Nucleus
CURRENCY SIGN clause	Nucleus
DECIMAL-POINT clause	Nucleus
Input-Output Section	
FILE-CONTROL paragraph	Sequential I-O
. . . .	Relative I-O
. . . .	Indexed I-O
. . . .	Sort-Merge
File control entry	Sequential I-O
. . . .	Relative I-O
. . . .	Indexed I-O
. . . .	Sort-Merge
SELECT clause	Sequential I-O
. . . .	Relative I-O
. . . .	Indexed I-O
. . . .	Sort-Merge

39

Elements	Module
ASSIGN clause	Sequential I-O
. . . .	Relative I-O
. . . .	Indexed I-O
. . . .	Sort-Merge
ORGANIZATION clause	
SEQUENTIAL	Sequential I-O
RELATIVE	Relative I-O
INDEXED	Indexed I-O
ACCESS MODE clause	
SEQUENTIAL	Sequential I-O
. . . .	Relative I-O
. . . .	Indexed I-O
RANDOM	Sequential I-O
. . . .	Relative I-O
. . . .	Indexed I-O
RECORD KEY clause	Indexed I-O
FILE STATUS clause	Sequential I-O
. . . .	Relative I-O
. . . .	Indexed I-O

Data Division

Communication Section	Communication
File Section	Sequential I-O
. . . .	Relative I-O
. . . .	Indexed I-O
. . . .	Sort-Merge
Linkage Section	IPC
Working-Storage Section	Nucleus
Communication description entry . . .	Communication
Data description entry	Nucleus
File description entry	Sequential I-O
. . . .	Relative I-O
. . . .	Indexed I-O
Record description entry	Sequential I-O
. . . .	Relative I-O
. . . .	Indexed I-O

Elements	*Module*
Sort-merge description entry	. Sort-Merge
BLOCK CONTAINS clause	
Integer RECORDS/CHARACTERS .	. Sequential I-O
. . . .	. Relative I-O
. . . .	. Indexed I-O
Data-name or FILLER clause	. Nucleus
LABEL RECORDS clause	. Sequential I-O
. . . .	. Relative I-O
. . . .	. Indexed I-O
Level-number	
01 through 10; must be 2 digits . . .	. Nucleus
OCCURS clause	. Table Handling
Integer TIMES	. Table Handling
PICTURE clause (or PIC clause) . . .	. Nucleus
Character-string may contain 30 characters	. Nucleus
Data characters: X 9	. Nucleus
Operational symbols: S V	. Nucleus
Fixed insertion characters B + − . , $	. Nucleus
Replacement or floating characters $ + − Z *	. Nucleus
Currency sign substitution	. Nucleus
Decimal point substitution	. Nucleus
REDEFINES clause: May not be nested	. Nucleus
SIGN clause	. Nucleus
SYNCHRONIZED clause (or SYNC clause)	Nucleus
USAGE clause	. Nucleus
DISPLAY	. Nucleus
COMPUTATIONAL (or COMP) . .	. Nucleus
VALUE clause	. Nucleus
Literal	. Nucleus
VALUE OF clause	
Implementor-name IS literal	. Sequential I-O
. . . .	. Relative I-O
. . . .	. Indexed I-O

Elements	*Module*

Procedure Division

Procedure Division header
  USING phrase; at least five data-names permitted . . . . IPC
Conditional expressions
  Simple condition . . . . Nucleus
    Relation condition . . . . Nucleus
      Relational operators
        [NOT] GREATER THAN . . . Nucleus
        [NOT] > . . . . Nucleus
        [NOT] LESS THAN . . . . Nucleus
        [NOT] < . . . . Nucleus
        [NOT] EQUAL TO . . . . . Nucleus
        [NOT] = ... Nucleus
      Comparison of numeric operands . . Nucleus
      Comparison of nonnumeric operands Nucleus
        Operands of unequal size are permitted Nucleus
    Class condition . . . . Nucleus
Arithmetic statements
  Arithmetic operands limited to 18 digits . Nucleus
ACCEPT statement
  Only one transfer of data . . . . . Nucleus
  MESSAGE COUNT phrase . . . . . Communication
ADD statement . . . . Nucleus
  TO identifier . . . . Nucleus
  GIVING identifier . . . . . . Nucleus
  ROUNDED phrase . . . . Nucleus
CALL statement . . . . IPC
  Literal . . . . IPC
  USING phrase; at least five data-names permitted . . . . IPC
CLOSE statement
  Single file-name . . . . Sequential I-O
  . . . . Relative I-O
  . . . . Indexed I-O

Elements	*Module*
DELETE statement	
INVALID KEY phrase	. Relative I-O
. . . .	. Indexed I-O
DISPLAY statement	. Nucleus
Only one transfer of data	. Nucleus
Identifier/literal	. Nucleus
DIVIDE statement	. Nucleus
BY identifier/literal	. Nucleus
GIVING identifier	. Nucleus
ROUNDED phrase	. Nucleus
EXIT PROGRAM statement	. IPC
GO TO statement	. Nucleus
Procedure-name is required	. Nucleus
DEPENDING ON phrase	. Nucleus
IF statement	. Nucleus
Limited to one or more imperative verbs	. Nucleus
ELSE phrase	. Nucleus
MOVE statement	. Nucleus
TO identifier	. Nucleus
MULTIPLY statement	. Nucleus
BY identifier	. Nucleus
GIVING identifier	. Nucleus
ROUNDED phrase	. Nucleus
OPEN statement	
Single file-name	. Sequential I-O
. . . .	. Relative I-O
. . . .	. Indexed I-O
INPUT phrase	. Sequential I-O
. . . .	. Relative I-O
. . . .	. Indexed I-O
OUTPUT phrase	. Sequential I-O
. . . .	. Relative I-O
. . . .	. Indexed I-O
I-O phrase	. Sequential I-O
. . . .	. Relative I-O
. . . .	. Indexed I-O

Elements	*Module*
PERFORM statement	Nucleus
Procedure-name	Nucleus
THRU phrase	Nucleus
TIMES phrase	Nucleus
UNTIL phrase	Nucleus
READ statement	
AT END phrase	Sequential I-O
	Relative I-O
	Indexed I-O
INVALID KEY phrase	Relative I-O
	Indexed I-O
RECEIVE statement	Communication
MESSAGE phrase	Communication
INTO identifier phrase	Communication
NO DATA phrase	Communication
RELEASE statement	Sort-Merge
RETURN statement	Sort-Merge
AT END phrase	Sort-Merge
REWRITE statement	Sequential I-O
	Relative I-O
	Indexed I-O
INVALID KEY phrase	Relative I-O
	Indexed I-O
SEND statement	Communication
FROM identifier phrase	Communication
WITH EMI phrase	Communication
WITH EGI phrase	Communication
BEFORE/AFTER ADVANCING phrase	Communication
Integer	Communication
Identifier	Communication
PAGE	Communication
SORT statement	Sort-Merge
Multiple SORT statements per program	Sort-Merge
KEY data-name	Sort-Merge
KEY data-name series	Sort-Merge
ASCENDING series	Sort-Merge

Elements	*Module*
DESCENDING series	Sort-Merge
Mixed ASCENDING/DESCENDING	Sort-Merge
INPUT PROCEDURE phrase	Sort-Merge
USING phrase	Sort-Merge
OUTPUT PROCEDURE phrase . . .	Sort-Merge
GIVING phrase	Sort-Merge
STOP statement	Nucleus
RUN	Nucleus
SUBTRACT statement	Nucleus
FROM identifier	Nucleus
GIVING identifier	Nucleus
ROUNDED phrase	Nucleus
WRITE statement	Sequential I-O
. . . .	Relative I-O
. . . .	Indexed I-O
BEFORE/AFTER ADVANCING phrase	Sequential I-O
integer	Sequential I-O
identifier	Sequential I-O
PAGE	Sequential I-O
INVALID KEY phrase	Relative I-O
. . . .	Indexed I-O

Segmentation

Segment-numbers 0 through 49 for permanent segments	Segmentation
Segment-numbers 50 through 99 for independent segments	Segmentation
All sections with the same segment-number must be together in the source program .	Segmentation

Library

COPY statement	Library

4

GLOSSARY

4.1 Introduction

The terms in this chapter are defined in accordance with their meaning as used in this document describing American National Standard Minimum COBOL and may not have the same meaning for other languages.

These definitions are also intended to be either reference material or introductory material to be reviewed prior to reading the detailed language specifications that follow. For this reason, these definitions are, in most instances, brief and do not include detailed syntactical rules.

4.2 Definitions

Access Mode. The manner in which records are to be operated upon within a file.

Actual Decimal Point. The physical representation, using either of the decimal point characters period (.) or comma (,), of the decimal point position in a data item.

Alphabetic Character. A character that belongs to the following set of letters: A, B, C, D, E, F, G, H, I, J, K, L, M, N, O, P, Q, R, S, T, U, V, W, X, Y, Z, and the space.

Alphanumeric Character. Any character in the computer's character set.

Ascending Key. A key upon the values of which data is ordered starting with the lowest value of key up to the highest value of key in accordance with the rules for comparing data items.

Assumed Decimal Point. A decimal point position which does not involve the existence of an actual character in a data item. The assumed decimal point has logical meaning but no physical representation.

At End Condition. A condition caused:

1. During the execution of a READ statement for a sequentially accessed file.

2. During the execution of a RETURN statement, when no next logical record exists for the associated sort file.

Block. A physical unit of data that is normally composed of one or more logical records. For mass storage files, a block may contain a portion of a logical record. The size of a block has no direct relationship to the size of the file within which the block is contained or to the size of the logical record(s) that are either continue within the block or that overlap the block. The term is synonymous with physical record.

Called Program. A program which is the object of a CALL statement combined at object time with the calling program to produce a run unit.

Calling Program. A program which executes a CALL to another program.

Cd-Name. A user-defined word that names an MCS interface area described in a communication description entry within the Communication Section of the Data Division.

Character. The basic indivisible unit of the language.

Character Position. A character position is the amount of physical storage required to store a single standard data form character described as usage in DISPLAY. Further characteristics of the physical storage are defined by the implementor.

Character-String. A sequence of contiguous characters which form a COBOL word, a literal, or a PICTURE character-string.

Class Condition. The proposition, for which a truth value can be determined, that the content of an item is wholly alphabetic or is wholly numeric.

Clause. A clause is an ordered set of consecutive COBOL character-strings whose purpose is to specify an attribute of an entry.

COBOL Character Set. The complete COBOL character set consists of the 51 characters listed below:

Character	*Meaning*
0, 1, . . . , 9	digit
A, B, . . . , Z	letter
	space (blank)
+	plus sign
−	minus sign (hyphen)
*	asterisk
/	stroke (virgule, slash)
=	equal sign
$	currency sign
,	comma (decimal point)
;	semicolon
.	period (decimal point)
"	quotation mark
(	left parenthesis
)	right parenthesis
>	greater than symbol
<	less than symbol

COBOL Word. (see Word)

Collating Sequence. The sequence in which the characters that are acceptable in a computer are ordered for purposes of sorting and comparing.

Comment Line. A source program line represented by an asterisk in the indicator area of the line and any characters from the computer's character set in area A and area B of that line. The comment line serves only for documentation in a program. A special form of comment line represented by a stroke (/) in the indicator area of the line and any characters from the computer's character set in area A and area B of that line causes page ejection prior to printing the comment.

Communication Description Entry. An entry in the Communication Section of the Data Division that is composed of the level indicator CD, followed by a cd-name, and then followed by a set of clauses as required. It describes the interface between the Message Control System (MCS) and the COBOL program.

Communication Device. A mechanism (hardware or hardware/software) capable of sending data to a queue and/or receiving data from a queue. This mechanism may be a computer or a peripheral device. One or more programs containing communication description entries and residing within the same computer define one or more of these mechanisms.

Communication Section. The section of the Data Division that describes the interface areas between the MCS and the program, composed of one or more CD description entries.

Compile Time. The time at which a COBOL source program is translated, by a COBOL compiler, to a COBOL object program.

Compiler Directing Statement. A statement, beginning with a compiler directing verb, that causes the compiler to take a specific action during compilation.

Computer-Name. A system-name that identifies the computer upon which the program is to be compiled or run.

Condition. A status of a program at execution time for which a truth value can be determined. Where the 'condition' (condition-1, condition-2, . . .) appears in these language specifications in or in reference to 'condition' (condition-1, condition-2, . . .) of a general format, it is a conditional expression consisting of a simple condition for which a truth value can be determined.

Conditional Expression. A simple condition specified in an IF or PERFORM statement. (see Simple Condition)

Conditional Statement. A conditional statement specifies that the truth value of a condition is to be determined and that the subsequent action of the object program is dependent on this truth value.

Configuration Section. A section of the Environment Division that describes overall specifications of source and object computers.

Connective. A reserved word that is used to link two or more operands written in a series.

Contiguous Items. Items that are described by consecutive entries in the Data Division, and that bear a definite hierarchic relationship to each other.

Currency Sign. The character '$' of the COBOL character set.

Currency Symbol. The character defined by the CURRENCY SIGN clause in the SPECIAL-NAMES paragraph. If no CURRENCY SIGN clause is present in a COBOL source program, the currency symbol is identical to the currency sign.

Current Record. The record which is available in the record area associated with the file.

Current Record Pointer. A conceptual entity that is used in the selection of the next record.

Data Clause. A clause that appears in a data description entry in the Data Division and provides information describing a particular attribute of a data item.

Data Description Entry. An entry in the Data Division that is composed of a level-number followed by a data-name, if required, and then followed by a set of data clauses, as required.

Data Item. A character or a set of contiguous characters (excluding in either case literals) defined as a unit of data by the COBOL program.

Data-Name. A user-defined word that names a data item described in a data description entry in the Data Division. When used in the general formats, 'data-name' represents a word which cannot be subscripted unless specifically permitted by the rules for that format.

Debugging Line. A debugging line is any line with 'D' in the indicator area of the line.

Descending Key. A key upon the values of which data is ordered starting with the highest value of key down to the lowest value of key, in accordance with the rules for comparing data items.

Destination. The symbolic identification of the receiver of a transmission from a queue.

Digit Position. A digit position is the amount of physical storage required to store a single digit. This amount may vary depending on the usage of the data item describing the digit position. Further characteristics of the physical storage are defined by the implementor.

Division. A set of zero, one or more sections of paragraphs, called the division body, that are formed and combined in accordance with a specific set of rules. These are four (4) divisions in a COBOL program: Identification, Environment, Data, and Procedure.

Division Header. A combination of words followed by a period and a space that indicates that beginning of a division. The division headers are:

IDENTIFICATION DIVISION.
ENVIRONMENT DIVISION.
DATA DIVISION.
PROCEDURE DIVISION [USING data-name-1
   [data-name-2] . . .].

Editing Character. A single character belonging to the following set:

Character	Meaning
B	space
+	plus
−	minus
Z	zero suppres
*	check protect
$	currency sign
,	comma (decimal point)
.	period (decimal point)

Elementary Item. A data item that is described as not being further logically subdivided.

End of Procedure Division. The physical position in a COBOL source program after which no further procedures appear.

Entry. Any descriptive set of consecutive clauses terminated by a period and written in the Environment Division or Data Division of a COBOL source program.

Environment Clause. A clause that appears as part of an Environment Division entry.

Execution Time. (see Object Time)

Figurative Constant. A compiler generated value referenced through the use of certain reserved words.

File. A collection of records.

File Clause. A clause that appears as part of any of the following Data Division entries:

File description (FD)
Sort-merge file description (SD)
Communication description (CD)

FILE-CONTROL. The name of an Environment Division paragraph in which the data files for a given source program are declared.

File Description Entry. An entry in the File Section of the Data Division that is composed of the level indicator FD, followed by a file-name, and then followed by a set of file clauses as required.

File-Name. A user-defined word that names a file described in a file description entry or a sort-merge file description entry within the File Section of the Data Division.

File Organization. The permanent logical file structure established at the time that a file is created.

File Section. The section of the Data Division that contains file description entries and sort-merge file description entries together with their associated record descriptions.

Format. A specific arrangement of a set of data.

Group Item. A named contiguous set of elementary or group items.

High Order End. The leftmost character of a string of characters.

I-O Mode. The state of a file after execution of an OPEN statement, with the I-O phrase specified, for that file and before the execution of a CLOSE statement for that file.

Identifier. A data-name, followed as required, by a subscript to make unique reference to a data item.

Imperative Statement. A statement that begins with an imperative verb and specifies an unconditional action to be taken. An imperative statement may consist of a sequence of imperative statements.

Implementor-Name. A system-name that refers to a particular feature available on that implementor's computing system.

Indexed File. A file with indexed organization.

Indexed Organization. The permanent logical file structure in which each record is identified by the value of one or more keys within that record.

Input File. A file that is opened in the input mode.

Input Mode. The state of a file after execution of an OPEN statement, with the INPUT phrase specified, for that file and before the execution of a CLOSE statement for that file.

Input-Output File. A file that is opened in the I-O mode.

Input-Output Section. The section of the Environment Division that names the files and the external media required by an object program and which provides information required for transmission and handling of data during execution of the object program.

Input Procedure. A set of statements that is executed each time a record is released to the sort files.

Integer. A numeric literal or a numeric data item that does not include any character positions to the right of the assumed decimal point. Where the term 'integer' appears in general formats, integer must not be a numeric data item, and must not be signed, nor zero unless explicitly allowed by the rules of that format.

Invalid Key Condition. A condition, at object time, caused when a specific value of the key associated with an indexes or relative file is determined to be invalid.

Key. A data item which identifies the location of a record, or a set of data items which serve to identify the ordering of data.

Key of Reference. The key currently being used to access records within an indexed file.

Key Word. A reserved word whose presence is required when the format in which the word appears is used in a source program.

Level Indicator. Two alphabetic characters that identify a specific type of file or a position in hierarchy.

Level-Number. A user-defined word which indicates the position of a data item in the hierarchical structure of a logical record. A level-number is expressed as a two digit number. Level-numbers in the range 1 through 10 indicate the position of a data item in the hierarchical structure of a logical record. Level-numbers in the range 1 through 9 must be written as a zero followed by a significant digit.

Library Text. A sequence of character-strings and/or separators in a COBOL library.

Linkage Section. The section in the Data Division of the called program that describes data items available from the calling program. These data items may be referred to by both the calling and called program.

Literal. A character-string whose value is implied by the ordered set of characters comprising the string.

Logical Record. The most inclusive data item. The Level number for a record is 01.

Low Order End. The rightmost character of a string of characters.

Mass Storage. A storage medium on which data may be organized and maintained in both a sequential and nonsequential manner.

Mass Storage Control System (MSCS). An input-output control system that directs, or controls, the processing of mass storage files.

Mass Storage File. A collection of records that is assigned to a mass storage medium.

MCS. (see Message Control System)

Message. Data associated with an end of message indicator or an end of group indicator. (See Message Indicators)

Message Control System (MCS). A communication control system that supports the processing of messages.

55

Message Count. The count of the number of complete messages that exist in the designated queue of messages.

Message Indicators. EGI (end of group indicator) and EMI (end of message indicator) are conceptual indications that serve to notify the MCS that a specific condition exists (end of group, end of message).

Within the hierarchy of EGI and EMI, an EGI is conceptually equivalent to an EMI and EGI. Thus, a message may be terminated by an EMI or EGI.

MSCS. (see Mass Storage Control System)

Next Executable Sentence. The next sentence to which control will be transferred after execution of the current statement is complete.

Next Executable Statement. The next statement to which control will be transferred after execution of the current statement is complete.

Next Record. The record which logically follows the current record of a file.

Noncontiguous Items. Elementary data items, in the Working-Storage and Linkage Sections, which bear no hierarchic relationship to other data items.

Nonnumeric Item. A data item whose description permits its contents to be composed of any combination of characters taken from the computer's character set. Certain categories of nonnumeric items may be formed from more restricted character sets.

Nonnumeric Literal. A character-string bounded by quotation marks. The string of characters may include any character in the computer's character set. To represent a single quotation mark character within a nonnumeric literal, two contiguous quotation marks must be used.

Numeric Character. A character that belongs to the following set of digits: 0, 1, 2, 3, 4, 5, 6, 7, 8, 9.

Numeric Item. A data item whose description restricts its contents to a value represented by characters chosen from the digits '0' through '9'; if signed, the item may also contain a '+', '−', or other representation of an operational sign.

Numeric Literal. A literal composed of one or more numeric characters that also may contain either a decimal point, or an algebraic sign, or both. The decimal point must not be the rightmost character. The algebraic sign, if present, must be the leftmost character.

OBJECT-COMPUTER. The name of an Environment Division paragraph in which the computer environment, within which the object program is executed, is described.

Object of Entry. A set of operands and reserved words, within a Data Division entry, that immediately follows the subject of the entry.

Object Program. A set or group of executable machine language instructions and other material designed to interact with data to provide problem solutions. In this context, an object program is generally the machine language result of the operation of a COBOL compiler on a source program. Where there is no danger of ambiguity, the word 'program' alone may be used in place of the phrase 'object program'.

Object Time. The time at which an object program is executed.

Open Mode. The state of a file after execution of an OPEN statement for that file and before the execution of a CLOSE statement for that file. The particular open mode is specified in the OPEN statement as either INPUT, OUTPUT, or I-O.

Operand. Whereas the general definition of operand is 'that component which is operated upon', for the purposes of this publication, any lowercase word (or words) that appears in a statement or entry format may be considered to be an operand and, as such, is an implied reference to the data indicated by the operand.

Operational Sign. An algebraic sign, associated with a numeric data item or a numeric literal, to indicate whether its value is positive or negative.

Optional Word. A reserved word that is included in a specific format only to improve the readability of the language and whose presence is optional to the user when the format in which the word appears is used in a source program.

Output File. A file that is opened in the output mode.

Output Mode. The state of a file after execution of an OPEN statement, with the OUTPUT phrase specified for that file and before the execution of a CLOSE statement for that file.

Output Procedure. A set of statements to which control is given during execution of a SORT statement after the sort function is completed.

Paragraph. In the Procedure Division, a paragraph-name followed by a period and a space and by zero, one, or more sentences. In the Identification and Environment Divisions, a paragraph header followed by zero, one, or more entries.

Paragraph Header. A reserved word, followed by a period and a space that indicates the beginning of a paragraph in the Identification and Environment Divisions. The permissible paragraph headers are:

In the Identification Division:

PROGRAM-ID

In the Environment Division:

SOURCE-COMPUTER.
OBJECT-COMPUTER.
SPECIAL-NAMES.
FILE-CONTROL.

Paragraph-Name. A user-defined word that identifies and begins a paragraph in the Procedure Division.

Phrase. A phrase is an ordered set of one or more consecutive COBOL character-strings that form a portion of a COBOL procedural statement or of a COBOL clause.

Physical Record. (see Block)

Prime Record Key. A key whose contents uniquely identify a record within an indexed file.

Procedure. A paragraph or group of logically successive paragraphs, or a section or group of logically successive sections, within the Procedure Division.

Procedure-Name. A user-defined word which is used to name a paragraph or section in the Procedure Division. It consists of a paragraph-name or a section-name.

Program-Name. A user-defined word that identifies a COBOL source program.

Punctuation Character. A character that belongs to the following set:

Character	Meaning
,	comma
;	semicolon
.	period
"	quotation mark
(	left parenthesis
)	right parenthesis
	space
=	equal sign

Queue. A logical collection of messages awaiting transmission or processing.

Queue Name. A symbolic name that indicates to the MCS the logical path by which a message may be accessible in a queue.

Random Access. An access mode in which the program-specified value of a key data item identifies the logical record that is obtained from, deleted from or placed into a relative or indexed file.

Record. (see Logical Record)

Record Area. A storage area allocated for the purpose of processing the record described in a record description entry in the File Section.

Record Description. (see Record Description Entry)

Record Description Entry. The total set of data description entries associated with a particular record.

Record Key. A key, the prime record key, whose contents identify a record within an indexed file.

Record-Name. A user-defined word that names a record described in a record description entry in the Data Division.

Reference Format. A format that provides a standard method for describing COBOL source programs.

Relation. (see Relational Operator)

Relation Character. A character that belongs to the following set:

Character	*Meaning*
>	greater than
<	less than
=	equal to

Relation Condition. The proposition, for which a truth value can be determined, that the value of a data item has a specific relationship to the value of another data item. (see Relational Operator)

Relational Operator. A reserved word, a relation character, a group of consecutive reserved words, or a group of consecutive reserved words and relation characters used in the construction of a relation condition. The permissible operators and their meaning are:

Relational Operator	*Meaning*
IS [NOT] GREATER THAN⎤ IS [NOT] > ⎦	Greater than or not greater than
IS [NOT] LESS THAN⎤ IS [NOT] < ⎦	Less than or not less than
IS [NOT] EQUAL TO⎤ IS [NOT] = ⎦	Equal to or not equal to

Relative File. A file with relative organization.

Relative Key. A key whose contents identify a logical record in a relative file.

Relative Organization. The permanent logical file structure in which each record is uniquely identified by an integer value greater than zero, which specifies the record's logical ordinal position in the file.

Reserved Word. A COBOL word specified in the list of words which may be used in the COBOL source programs, but which must not appear in the programs as user-defined words or system-names.

Run Unit. A set of one or more object programs which function, at object time, as a unit to provide problem solutions.

Section. A set of zero, one, or more paragraphs or entries, called a section body, the first of which is preceded by a section header. Each section consists of the section header and the related section body.

Section Header. A combination of words followed by a period and a space that indicates the beginning of a section in the Environment, Data and Procedure Division.

In the Environment and Data Divisions, a section header is composed of reserved words followed by a period and a space. The permissible section headers are:

In the Environment Division:

CONFIGURATION SECTION.
INPUT-OUTPUT SECTION.

In the Data Division:

FILE SECTION.
WORKING-STORAGE SECTION.
LINKAGE SECTION.
COMMUNICATION SECTION.

In the Procedure Division, a section header is composed of a section-name, followed by the reserved word SECTION, followed by a segment-number (optional), followed by a period and a space.

Section-Name. A user-defined word which names a section in the Procedure Division.

Segment-Number. A user-defined word which classifies sections in the Procedure Division for purposes of segmentation. Segment-numbers may contain only the characters '0', '1', . . ., '9'. A segment-number may be expressed either as a one or two digit number.

Sentence. A sequence of one or more statements, the last of which is terminated by a period followed by a space.

Separator. A punctuation character used to delimit character-strings.

Sequential Access. An access mode in which logical records are obtained from or placed into a file in a consecutive predecessor-to-successor logical record sequence determined by the order of records in the file.

Sequential File. A file with sequential organization.

Sequential Organization. The permanent logical file structure in which a record is identified by a predecessor-successor relationship established when the record is placed into the file.

Simple Condition. Any single condition chosen from the set:
relation condition
class condition

Sort File. A collection of records to be sorted by a SORT statement. The sort file is created and can be used by the sort function only.

Sort-Merge File Description Entry. An entry in the File Section of the Data Division that is composed of the level indicator SD, followed by a file-name, and then followed by a set of file clauses as required.

Source. The symbolic identification of the originator of a transmission to a queue.

SOURCE-COMPUTER. The name of an Environment Division paragraph in which the computer environment, within which the source program is compiled, is described.

Source Program. Although it is recognized that a source program may be represented by other forms and symbols, in this document it always refers to a syntactically correct set of COBOL statements beginning with an Identification Division and ending with the end of the Procedure Division. In contexts where there is no danger of ambiguity, the word 'program' alone may be used in place of the phrase 'source program'.

Special Character. A character that belongs to the following set:

Character	Meaning
+	plus sign
−	minus sign
*	asterisk
/	stroke (virgule, slash)
=	equal sign
$	currency sign
,	comma (decimal point)
;	semicolon
.	period (decimal point)
"	quotation mark

(	left parenthesis
)	right parenthesis
>	greater than symbol
<	less than symbol

Special-Character Word. A reserved word which is a relation character.

SPECIAL-NAMES. The name of an Environment Division paragraph which provides a means of specifying the character to represent the currency symbol and of interchanging the function of the comma and period in the PICTURE character-string.

Standard Data Format. The concept used in describing the characteristics of data in a COBOL Data Division under which the characteristics or properties of the data are expressed in a form oriented to the appearance of the data on a printed page of infinite length and breadth, rather than a form oriented to the manner in which the data is stored internally in the computer, or on a particular external medium.

Statement. A syntactically valid combination of words and symbols written in the Procedure Division beginning with a verb.

Subject of Entry. An operand or reserved word that appears immediately following the level indicator or the level-number in a Data Division entry.

Subprogram. (see Called Program)

Subscript. An integer whose value identifies a particular element in a table.

Subscripted Data-Name. An identifier that is composed of a data-name followed by a subscript enclosed in parenthesis.

System-Name. A COBOL word which is used to communicate with the operating environment.

Table. A set of logically consecutive items of data that are defined in the Data Division by means of the OCCURS clause.

Table Element. A data item that belongs to the set of repeated items comprising a table.

Text-Name. A user-defined word which identifies library text.

Truth Value. The representation of the result of the evaluation of a condition in terms of one of two values: true, false.

Unit. A module of mass storage the dimensions of which are determined by each implementor.

User-Defined Word. A COBOL word that must be supplied by the user to satisfy the format of a clause or statement.

Verb. A word that expresses an action to be taken by a COBOL compiler or object program.

Word. A character-string of not more than 30 characters which forms a user-defined word, a system-name, or a reserved word.

Working-Storage Section. The section of the Data Division that describes working storage data items, composed either of noncontiguous items or of working storage records or of both.

5

OVERALL LANGUAGE CONSIDERATION

5.1 Introduction

The language considerations and rules specified in this chapter, apply to all elements within American National Standard Minimum COBOL. When a particular module does not allow all of these language concepts, the restriction will be pointed out in the chapter describing that language element. It should be noted that restrictions contained in one module apply to other modules when implemented together. For example, data-names must begin with an alphabetic character in the Nucleus; therefore, any module combined with Nucleus would have the same restriction.

5.2 Notation Used in Formats and Rules

5.2.1 DEFINITION OF A GENERAL FORMAT

A general format is the specific arrangement of the elements of a clause or a statement. A clause or a statement consists of elements as defined below. Throughout this document, a format is shown adjacent to information defining the clause or statement. When more than one specific arrangement is permitted, the general format is separated into numbered formats. (Clauses that are optional must appear in the sequence shown if they are used.) In certain cases, stated explicitly in the rules associated with a given format, the clauses may appear in sequences other than that shown. Applications, requirements or restrictions are shown as rules.

5.2.1.1 Syntax Rules

Syntax rules are those rules that define or clarify the order in which words or elements are arranged to form larger elements such as phrases, clauses, or statements. Syntax rules also impose restrictions on individual words or elements.

These rules are used to define or clarify how the statement must be written, i.e., the order of the elements of the statement and restrictions on what each element may represent.

5.2.1.2 General Rules

A general rule is a rule that defines or clarifies the meaning or relationship of meanings of an element or set of elements. It is used to define or clarify the semantics of the statement and the effect that it has on either execution or compilation.

5.2.1.3 Elements

Elements which make up a clause or a statement consist of uppercase words, lowercase words, level-numbers, brackets, braces, connectives and special characters.

5.2.1.4 Words

All underlined uppercase words are called key words and are required when the functions of which they are a part are used. Uppercase words which are not underlined are optional to the user and may or may not be present in the source program. Uppercase words, whether underlined or not, must be spelled correctly.

Lowercase words, in a general format, are generic terms used to represent COBOL words, literals, PICTURE character-strings, or a complete syntactical entry that must be supplied by the user. Where generic terms are repeated in a general format, a number or letter appendage to the term serves to identify that term for explanation or discussion.

5.2.1.5 Level-Numbers

When specific level-numbers appear in data description entry formats, those specific level-numbers are required when such entries are used in a COBOL program.

5.2.1.6 Brackets and Braces

When a portion of a general format is enclosed in brackets, [ ], that portion may be included or omitted at the user's choice. Braces, { } , enclosing a portion of a general format means a selection of one of the options contained within the braces must be made. In both cases, a choice is indicated by vertically stacking the possibilities. When brackets or braces enclose a portion of a format, but only one possibility is shown, the function of the brackets or braces is to delimit that portion of the format to which a following ellipsis applies. (See paragraph 5.2.1.7, The Ellipsis.) If an option within braces contains only reserved words that are not key words, then the option is a default option (implicitly selected unless one of the other options is explicitly indicated).

5.2.1.7 The Ellipsis

In text, the ellipsis (. . .) may show the omission of a portion of a source program. This meaning becomes apparent in context.

In the general formats, the ellipsis represents the position at which repetition may occur at the user's option. The portion of the format that may be repeated is determined as follows:

Given . . . in a clause or statement format, scanning right to left, determine the] or } immediately to the left of the . . . ; continue scanning right to left and determine the logically matching [or { ; the . . . applies to the words between the determined pair of delimiters.

5.2.1.8 Format Punctuation

The punctuation characters comma and semicolon are shown in some formats. Where shown in the formats, they are optional and may be included or omitted by the user. In the source program these two punctuation characters are interchangeable and either one may be used anywhere one of them is shown in the formats. Neither one may appear immediately preceding the first clause of an entry of paragraph.

If desired, a semicolon or comma may be used between statements in the Procedure Division.

Paragraphs within the Identification and Procedure Division, and the entries within the Environment and Data Divisions must be terminated by the separator period.

5.2.1.9 Use of Certain Special Characters in Formats

The characters '>', '<', '=', when appearing in formats, although not underlined, are required when such formats are used.

5.3 Language Concepts

5.3.1 CHARACTER SET

The most basic and indivisible unit of the language is the character. The set of characters used to form COBOL character-strings and separators includes the letters of the alphabet, digits and special characters. The character set consists of 51 characters as defined under COBOL Character Set in the glossary in Chapter 4. In the case of nonnumeric literals and comment lines, the character set is expanded to include the computer's entire character set. The characters allowable in each type of character-string and as separators are defined in paragraph 5.3.2 and in the glossary beginning with paragraph 4.2.

Since the character set of a particular computer may not have the characters defined, single character substitution must be made as required. When such a character set contains fewer than 51 characters, double characters must be substituted for the single characters.

5.3.2 LANGUAGE STRUCTURE

The individual characters of the language are concatenated to form character-strings and separators. A separator may be concatenated with another separator or with a character-string. A character-string may only be concatenated with a separator. The concatenation of character-strings and separators forms the text of a source program.

5.3.2.1 Separators

A separator is a string of one or more punctuation characters. The rules for formation of separators are:

1. The punctuation character space is a separator. Anywhere a space is used as a separator, more than one space may be used.

2. The punctuation characters comma, semicolon and period, when immediately followed by a space, are separators. These separators may appear in a COBOL source program only where explicitly permitted by the general formats, by format punctuation rules (see paragraph 5.-2.1.8, Format Punctuation), by statement and sentence structure definitions (see paragraph 5.7.2, Statements and Sentences), or reference format rules (see paragraph 5.8, Reference Format).

3. The punctuation characters right and left parenthesis are separators. Parentheses may appear only in balanced pairs of left and right parentheses delimiting subscripts.

4. The punctuation character quotation mark is a separator. An opening quotation mark must be immediately preceded by a space or left parenthesis; a closing quotation mark must be immediately followed by one of the separators space, comma, semicolon, period, or right parenthesis.

   Quotation marks may appear only in balanced pairs delimiting nonnumeric literals except when the literal is continued. (See paragraph 5.8.2.2., Continuation of Lines.)

5. The separator space may optionally immediately precede all separators except:

   a. As specified by reference format rules (see paragraph 5.8, Reference Format), and

   b. The separator closing quotation mark. In this case, a preceding space is considered as part of the nonnumeric literal and not as a separator.

6. The separator space may optionally immediately follow any separator except the opening quotation mark. In this case, a following space is considered as part of the nonnumeric literal and not as a separator.

Any punctuation character which appears as part of the specification of a PICTURE character-string or numeric literal is not considered as a punctuation character, but rather as a symbol used in the specification of that PICTURE character-string or numeric literal. PICTURE character-strings are delimited only by the separators space, comma, semicolon, or period.

The rules established for the formation of separators do not apply to the characters which comprise the contents of nonnumeric literals or comment lines.

5.3.2.2 Character-Strings

A character-string is a character or a sequence of contiguous characters which forms a COBOL word, a literal, or a PICTURE character-string. A character-string is delimited by separators.

5.3.2.2.1 COBOL WORDS

A COBOL word is a character-string of not more than 15 characters which forms a user-defined word, a system-name, or a reserved word. Within a given source program these classes form disjoint sets; a COBOL word may belong to one and only one of these classes.

5.3.2.2.1.1 *User-Defined Words.* A user-defined word is a COBOL word that must be supplied by the user to satisfy the format of a clause or statement. Each character of a user-defined word is selected from the set of characters 'A', 'B', 'C', . . . 'Z', '0', . . . '9', and '—', except that the '—' may not appear as the first or last character.

There are ten (10) types of user-defined words:

cd-name
data-name
file-name
level-number
paragraph-name
program-name
record-name
section-name
segment-number
text-name

Within a given source program, eight (8) of these ten (10) types of user-defined words are grouped into seven (7) disjoint sets. The disjoint sets are:

cd-names
data-names and record-names
file-names
paragraph-names
program-names
section-names
text-names

All user-defined words, except segment-numbers and level-numbers, can belong to one and only one of these disjoint sets. Further, all user-defined words within a given disjoint set must be unique because no other user-defined word in the same source program has identical spelling or punctuation.

With the exception of paragraph-name, section-name, level-number, and segment-number, all user-defined words must contain at least one alphabetic character. Segment-numbers and level-numbers need not be unique; a given specification of a segment-number or level-number may be identical to any other segment-number or level-number and may even be identical to a paragraph-name or section-name.

5.3.2.2.1.1.1 PARAGRAPH-NAMES. A paragraph-name is a word which names a paragraph in the Procedure Division. Paragraph-names are equivalent if, and only if, they are composed of the same sequence of the same number of digits and/or characters.

5.3.2.2.1.1.2 SECTION-NAMES. A section-name is a word which names a section in the Procedure Division. Section-names are equivalent if, and only if, they are composed of the same sequence of the same number of digits and/or characters.

5.3.2.2.1.1.3 OTHER USER-DEFINED NAMES. See the glossary beginning with paragraph 4.2 for definitions of all other types of user-defined words.

5.3.2.2.1.2 *System-Names.* A system-name is a COBOL word which is used to communicate with the operating environment. Rules for the formation of a system-name are defined by the implementor, except that each character used in the formation of a system-name must be selected from the set of characters 'A', 'B', 'C', ... 'Z', '0', ... '9', and '—', except that the '—' may not appear as the first or last character.

There are two (2) types of system-names:

computer-name
implementor-name

Within a given implementation these two types of system-names form disjoint sets; a given system-name may belong to one and only one of them. The system-names listed above are individually defined in the glossary in Chapter 4.

5.3.2.2.1.3 *Reserved Words.* A reserved word is a COBOL word that is one of the specified list of words which may be used in COBOL source programs, but which must not appear in the programs as user-defined words or system-names. Reserved words can only be used as specified in the general formats. (See paragraph 5.9, Reserved Words.)

There are four (4) types of reserved words:

Key words
Optional words
Connectives
Special-character words

5.3.2.2.1.3.1 KEY WORDS. A key word is a word whose presence is required when the format in which the word appears is used in a source program. Within each format, such words are uppercase and underlined.

Key words are of three types:

1. Verbs such as ADD and READ.
2. Required words, which appear in statement and entry formats.
3. Words which have a specific functional meaning such as SECTION.

5.3.2.2.1.3.2 OPTIONAL WORDS. Within each format, uppercase words that are not underlined are called optional words and may appear at the user's option. The presence or absence of an optional word does not alter the semantics of the COBOL program in which it appears.

5.3.2.2.1.3.3 CONNECTIVES. There is one type of connective:

1. Series connectives that link two or more consecutive operands: , (separator comma) or ; (separator semicolon)

5.3.2.2.1.3.4 FIGURATIVE CONSTANTS. Certain reserved words are used to name and reference specific constant values. These reserved words are specified paragraph 5.3.2.2.2.3, Figurative Constant Values.

5.3.2.2.1.3.5 SPECIAL-CHARACTER WORDS. The relation characters are reserved words. (See the glossary beginning with paragraph 4.2.)

5.3.2.2.2 LITERALS

A literal is a character-string whose value is implied by an ordered set of characters of which the literal is composed or by specification of a reserved word which references a figurative constant. Every literal belongs to one of two types, nonnumeric or numeric.

5.3.2.2.2.1 *Nonnumeric Literals.* A nonnumeric literal is a character-string delimited on both ends by quotation marks and consisting of any allowable character in the computer's character set. The implementor must allow for nonnumeric literals of 1 through 120 characters in length. To represent a single quotation mark character within a nonnumeric literal, two contiguous quotation marks must be used. The value of a nonnumeric literal in the object program is the string of characters itself, except:

1. The delimiting quotation marks are excluded, and
2. Each embedded pair of contiguous quotation marks represents a single quotation mark character.

All other punctuation characters are part of the value of the nonnumeric literal rather than separators; all nonnumeric literals are category alphanumeric. (See page 124, The PICTURE Clause.)

5.3.2.2.2.2 *Numeric Literals.* A numeric literal is a character-string whose characters are selected from the digits '0' through '9', the plus sign, the minus sign, and/or the decimal point. The implementor must allow for numeric literals of 1 through 18 digits in length. The rules for the formation of numeric literals are as follows:

1. A literal must contain at least one digit.
2. A literal must not contain more than one sign character. If a sign is used, it must appear as the leftmost character of the literal. If the literal is unsigned, the literal is positive.
3. A literal must not contain more than one decimal point. The decimal point is treated as an assumed decimal point,

and may appear anywhere within the literal except as the rightmost character. If the literal contains no decimal point, the literal is an integer.

If a literal conforms to the rules for the formation of numeric literals, but is enclosed in quotation marks, it is a nonnumeric literal and it is treated as such by the compiler.

4. The value of a numeric literal is the algebraic quantity represented by the characters in the numeric literal. Every numeric literal is category numeric. (See Section II, paragraph 4.5, The PICTURE Clause.) The size of a numeric literal in standard data format characters is equal to the number of digits specified by the user.

5.3.2.2.2.3 *Figurative Constant Values.* Figurative constant values are generated by the compiler and referenced through the use of the reserved words given below. These words must not be bounded by quotation marks when used as figurative constants. The single and plural forms of figurative constants are equivalent and may be used interchangeably.

The figurative constant values and the reserved words used to reference them are as follows:

ZERO ZEROS ZEROES	Represents the value '0', or one or more of the character '0', depending on context.
SPACE SPACES	Represents one or more of the character space from the computer's character set.

When a figurative constant represents a string of one or more characters, the length of the string is determined by the compiler from context according to the following rules:

1. When a figurative constant is associated with another data item, as when the figurative constant is moved to or compared with another data item, the string of characters specified by the figurative constant is repeated character by character on the right until the size of the resultant

string is equal to the size in characters of the associated data item.

2. When a figurative constant is not associated with another data item, as when the figurative constant appears in a DISPLAY statement, the length of the string is one character.

A figurative constant may be used wherever a literal appears in a format, except that whenever the literal is restricted to having only numeric characters in it, the only figurative constant permitted is ZERO (ZEROS, ZEROES).

Each reserved word which is used to reference a figurative constant value is a distinct character-string.

5.3.2.2.2.4 *PICTURE Character-String.* A PICTURE character-string consists of certain combinations of characters in the COBOL character set used as symbols. See page 124, The PICTURE Clause, for the discussion of the PICTURE character-string and for the rules that govern their use.

Any punctuation character which appears as part of the specification of a PICTURE character-string is not considered as a punctuation character, but rather as a symbol used in the specification of that PICTURE character-string.

5.3.3 CONCEPT OF COMPUTER INDEPENDENT DATA DESCRIPTION

To make data as computer independent as possible, the characteristics or properties of the data are described in relation to a standard data format rather than an equipment-oriented format. This standard data format is oriented to general data processing applications and uses the decimal system to represent numbers (regardless of the radix used by the computer) and the remaining characters in the COBOL character set to describe nonnumeric data items.

5.3.3.1 Logical Record and File Concept

The approach taken in defining file information is to distinguish between the physical aspects of the file and the conceptual characteristics of the data contained within the file.

5.3.3.1.1 PHYSICAL ASPECTS OF A FILE

The physical aspects of a file describe the data as it appears on the input or output media and include such features as:

1. The grouping of logical records within the physical limitations of the file medium.

2. The means by which the file can be identified.

5.3.3.1.2 CONCEPTUAL CHARACTERISTICS OF A FILE

The conceptual characteristics of a file are the explicit definition of each logical entity within the file itself. In a COBOL program, the input or output statements refer to one logical record.

It is important to distinguish between a physical record and a logical record. A COBOL logical record is a group of related information, uniquely identifiable, and treated as a unit.

A physical record is a physical unit of information whose size and recording mode is convenient to a particular computer for the storage of data on an input or output device. The size of a physical record is hardware dependent and bears no direct relationship to the size of the file of information contained on a device.

A logical record may be contained within a single physical unit; or several logical records may be contained within a single physical unit; or, in the case of mass storage files, a logical record may require more than one physical unit to contain it. There are several source language methods available for describing the relationship of logical records and physical units. When a permissible relationship has been established, control of the accessibility of logical records as related to the physical unit must be provided by the interaction of the object program on the implementor's hardware and/or software system. In this document, references to records means to logical records, unless the term 'physical record' is specifically used.

The concept of a logical record is not restricted to file data but is carried over into the definition of working storage. Thus, working storage may be grouped into logical records and defined by a series of record description entries.

5.3.3.1.3 RECORD CONCEPTS

The record description consists of a set of data description entries which describe the characteristics of a particular record. Each data description entry consists of a level-number followed by a data-name, if required, followed by a series of independent clauses, as required.

5.3.3.2 Concept of Levels

A level concept is inherent in the structure of a logical record. This concept arises from the need to specify subdivisions of a record for the purpose of data reference. Once a subdivision has been specified, it may be further subdivided to permit more detailed data referral.

The most basic subdivisions of a record, that is, those not further subdivided, are called elementary items; consequently, a record is said to consist of a sequence of elementary items, or the record itself may be an elementary item.

In order to refer to a set of elementary items, the elementary items are combined into groups. Each group consists of a named sequence of one or more elementary items. Groups, in turn, may be combined into groups of two or more groups, etc. Thus, an elementary item may belong to more than one group.

5.3.3.2.1 LEVEL-NUMBERS

A system of level-numbers shows the organization of elementary items and group items. Since records are the most inclusive data items, level-numbers for records start at 01. Less inclusive data items are assigned higher (not necessarily successive) level-numbers not greater in value than 10. Separate entries are written in the source program for each level-number used.

A group includes all group and elementary items following it until a level-number less than or equal to the level-number of that group is encountered. All items which are immediately subordinate to a given group item must be described using identical level-numbers greater than the level-number used to describe that group item.

5.3.3.3 Concept of Classes of Data

The four categories of data items (see Section II, paragraph 4.5, The PICTURE Clause) are grouped into two classes: numeric and alphanumeric. For numeric, the classes and categories are synonymous. The alphanumeric class includes the categories of alphanumeric edited, numeric edited, and alphanumeric (without editing). Every elementary item except for an index data item belongs to one of the classes and further to one of the categories. The class of a group item is treated at object time as alphanumeric regardless of the class of elementary items subordinate to that group item. Table 2 depicts the relationship of the class and categories of data items.

Table 2

Level of Item	Class	Category
	Numeric	*Numeric*
Elementary	Alphanumeric	Numeric Edited Alphanumeric Edited Alphanumeric
Nonelementary (Group)	Alphanumeric	Numeric Numeric Edited Alphanumeric Edited Alphanumeric

5.3.3.4 Selection of Character Representation and Radix

The value of a numeric item may be represented in either binary or decimal form depending on the equipment. In addition there are several ways of expressing decimal. Since these representations are actually combinations of bits, they are commonly called binary-coded decimal forms. The selection of radix is generally dependent upon the arithmetic capability of the computer. If more than one arithmetic radix is provided, the selection is dependent upon factors included in such clauses as USAGE. The binary-coded decimal form is also used to represent characters and symbols that are alphanumeric items.

The selection of the proper binary-coded alphanumeric or binary-coded decimal form is dependent upon the capability of the computer and its external media.

When a computer provides more than one means of representing data, the standard data format must be used if not otherwise specified by the data description. If both the external medium and the computer are capable of handling more than one form of data representation, or if there is no external medium associated with the data, the selection is dependent on factors included in USAGE, PICTURE, etc., clauses. Each implementor provides a complete explanation of the possible forms on the computer for which he is implementing COBOL. The method used in selecting the proper data form is also provided to allow the programmer to anticipate and/or control the selection.

The size of an elementary data item or a group item is the number of characters in standard data format of the item. Synchronization and usage may cause a difference between this size and the actual number of characters required for the internal representation.

5.3.3.5 Algebraic Signs

Algebraic signs are of two categories: operational signs, which are associated with signed numeric data items and signed numeric literals to indicate their algebraic properties; and editing signs, which appear on edited reports to identify the sign of the item.

The SIGN clause permits the programmer to state explicitly the location of the operational sign. The clause is optional; if it is not used operational signs will be represented as defined by the implementor.

Editing signs are inserted into a data item through the use of the sign control symbols of the PICTURE clause.

5.3.3.6 Standard Alignment Rules

The standard rules for positioning data within an elementary item depend on the category of the receiving item. These rules are:

1. If the receiving data item is described as numeric:
   a. The data is aligned by decimal point and is moved to the receiving character positions with zero fill or truncation on either end as required.
   b. When an assumed decimal point is not explicitly specified, the data item is treated as if it had an assumed decimal point immediately following its rightmost character and is aligned as in paragraph 1a above.

2. If the receiving data item is a numeric edited data item, the data moved to the edited data item is aligned by decimal point with zero fill or truncation at either end as required within the receiving character positions of the data item, except where editing requirements cause replacement of the leading zeros.

3. If the receiving data item is alphanumeric (other than a numeric edited data item) or alphanumeric edited, the sending data is moved to the receiving character positions and aligned at the leftmost character position in the data item with space fill or truncation to the right, as required.

5.3.3.7 Item Alignment for Increased Object-Code Efficiency

Some computer memories are organized in such a way that there are natural addressing boundaries in the computer memory (e.g., word boundaries, half-word boundaries, byte boundaries). The way in which data is stored is determined by the object program, and need not respect these natural boundaries.

However, certain uses of data (e.g., in arithmetic operations or in subscripting) may be facilitated if the data is stored so as to be aligned on these natural boundaries. Specifically, additional machine operations in the object program may be required for the accessing and storage of data if portions of two or more data items appear between adjacent natural boundaries, or if certain natural boundaries bifuracte a single data item.

Data items which are aligned on these natural boundaries in such a way as to avoid such additional machine operations are defined to be synchronized. A synchronized item is assumed to be introduced and carried in that form; conversion to synchronized form occurs only during execution of a procedure (other than READ or WRITE) which stores data in the item.

Synchronization can be accomplished in two ways:

1. By use of the SYNCHRONIZED clause

2. By recognizing the appropriate natural boundaries and organizing the data suitably within the use of the SYN-CHRONIZED clause. (See page 137, The SYNCHRO-NIZED Clause, General Rule 9.)

Each implementor who provides for special types of alignment will specify the precise interpretations which are to be made.

5.3.3.8 Uniqueness of Reference

5.3.3.8.1 SUBSCRIPTING

Subscripts can be used only when reference is made to an individual element within a list or table of like elements that have not been assigned individual data-names (see page 170, The OC-CURS Clause).

The subscript can be represented either by a numeric literal that is an integer or by a data-name. The data-name must be a numeric elementary item that represents an integer.

The subscript may be signed and, if signed, it must be positive. The lowest possible subscript value is 1. This value points to the first element of the table. The next sequential elements of the table are pointed to by subscripts whose values are 2, 3, ... The highest permissible subscript value, in any particular case, is the maximum number of occurrences of the item as specified in the OCCURS clause.

The subscript that identifies the table element is delimited by the balanced pair of separators left parenthesis and right parenthesis following the table element data-name. The table element data-name appended with a subscript is called a subscripted data-name or an identifier.

The format is:

data-name (subscript)

5.3.3.8.2 IDENTIFIER

An identifier is a term used to reflect that a data-name, if not unique in a program, must be followed by a subscript necessary to ensure uniqueness.

The general format for an identifier is:

data-name (subscript)

The restriction on subscripting is:

1. A data-name must not itself be subscripted when that data-name is being used as a subscript.

5.3.4 EXPLICIT AND IMPLICIT SPECIFICATIONS

There are three types of explicit and implicit specifications that occur in COBOL source programs:

1. Explicit and implicit Procedure Division references
2. Explicit and implicit transfers of control
3. Explicit and implicit attributes.

5.3.4.1 Explicit and Implicit Procedure Division References

A COBOL source program can reference data items either explicitly or implicitly in Procedure Division statements. An explicit reference occurs when the name of the referenced item is written in a Procedure Division statement. An implicit reference occurs when the item is referenced by a Procedure Division statement without the name of the referenced item being written in the source statement. An implicit reference also occurs, during the execution of a PERFORM statement, when the index or data item referenced by the index-name or identifier specified in the UNTIL phrase is evaluated by the control mechanism associated with that PERFORM statement. Such an implicit reference occurs if and only if the data item contributes to the execution of the statement.

5.3.4.2 Explicit and Implicit Transfers of Control

The mechanism that controls program flow transfers control from statement to statement in the sequence in which they were written in the source program unless an explicit transfer of control overrides this sequence or there is no next executable statement to which control can be passed. The transfer of control from statement to statement occurs without the writing of an explicit Procedure Division statement, and therefore, is an implicit transfer of control.

COBOL provides both explicit and implicit means of altering the implicit control transfer mechanism.

In addition to the implicit transfer of control between consecutive statements, implicit transfer of control also occurs when the normal flow is altered without the execution of a procedure branching statement. COBOL provides the following types of implicit control flow alterations which override the statement-to-statement transfers of control:

1. If a paragraph is being executed under control of another COBOL statement (for example, PERFORM and SORT) and the paragraph is the last paragraph in the range of the controlling statement, then an implied transfer of control

occurs from the last statement in the paragraph to the control mechanism of the last executed controlling statement. Further, if a paragraph is being executed under the control of a PERFORM statement which causes iterative execution and that paragraph is the first paragraph in the range of that PERFORM statement, an implicit transfer of control occurs between the control mechanism associated with that PERFORM statement and the first statement in that paragraph for each iterative execution of the paragraph.

2. When a SORT statement is executed, an implicit transfer of control occurs to any associated input or output procedures.

An explicit transfer of control consists of an alteration of the implicit control transfer mechanism by the execution of a procedure branching or conditional statement. (See paragraph 5.7.2.4, Categories of Statements.) An explicit transfer of control can be caused only by the execution of a procedure branching or conditional statement. The procedure branching statement EXIT PROGRAM causes an explicit transfer of control when the statement is executed in a called program.

In this document, the term 'next executable statement' is used to refer to the next COBOL statement to which control is transferred according to the rules above and the rules associated with each language element in the Procedure Division.

There is no next executable statement following:

1. The last statement in a program when the paragraph in which it appears is not being executed under the control of some other COBOL statement.

5.3.4.3 Explicit and Implicit Attributes

Attributes may be implicitly or explicitly specified. Any attribute which has been explicitly specified is called an explicit attribute. If an attribute has not been specified explicitly, then the attribute takes on the default specification. Such an attribute is known as an implicit attribute.

For example, the usage of a data item need not be specified, in which case a data item's usage is DISPLAY.

5.4 Identification Division

5.4.1 GENERAL DESCRIPTION

The Identification Division must be included in every COBOL source program. This division identifies both the source program and the resultant output listing.

5.4.2 ORGANIZATION

A paragraph header identifies the type of information contained in the paragraph. The name of the program must be given in the paragraph which is the PROGRAM-ID paragraph.

5.4.3 STRUCTURE

The following is the general format of the paragraph in the Identification Division.

5.4.3.1 General Format

IDENTIFICATION DIVISION.
PROGRAM-ID. program-name.

5.5 Environment Division

5.5.1 GENERAL DESCRIPTION

The Environment Division specifies a standard method of expression those aspects of a data processing problem that are dependent upon the physical characteristics of a specific computer. This division allows specification of the configuration of the compiling computer and the object computer. In addition, information relating to input-output control, and control techniques can be given.

The Environment Division must be included in every COBOL source program.

5.5.2 ORGANIZATION

Two sections make up the Environment Division: the Configuration Section and the Input-Output Section.

The Configuration Section deals with the characteristics of the source computer and the object computer. This section is divided into three paragraphs: the SOURCE-COMPUTER paragraph, which describes the computer configuration on which the source program is compiled; the OBJECT-COMPUTER paragraph, which describes the computer configuration on which the object program produced by the compiler is to be run; and the SPECIAL-NAMES paragraph, which specifies the character to represent the currency symbol and/or interchanges the functions of the comma and period in the PICTURE character-string and in numeric literals.

The Input-Output Section deals with the information needed to control transmission and handling of data between external media and the object program. This section contains the FILE-CONTROL paragraph which names and associates the files with external media.

5.5.3 STRUCTURE

The following is the general format of the sections and paragraphs in the Environment Division, and defines the order of presentation in the source program.

5.5.3.1 General Format

ENVIRONMENT DIVISION.
CONFIGURATION SECTION.
SOURCE-COMPUTER. source-computer-entry

OBJECT-COMPUTER. object-computer-entry

[SPECIAL-NAMES. special-names-entry]

[INPUT-OUTPUT SECTION.

FILE-CONTROL. {file-control-entry} . . .]

5.5.3.2 Syntax Rules

(1) The Environment Division begins with the reserved words
ENVIRONMENT DIVISION followed by a period and a space.

5.6 Data Division

5.6.1 OVERALL APPROACH

The Data Division describes the data that the object program
is to accept as input, to manipulate, to create, or to produce as
output. Data to be processed falls into three categories:

1. That which is contained in files and enters or leaves the
   internal memory of the computer from a specified area or
   areas.
2. That which is developed internally and placed into inter-
   mediate or working storage.
3. Constants which are defined by the user.

5.6.2 PHYSICAL AND LOGICAL ASPECTS OF DATA DESCRIPTION

5.6.2.1 Data Division Organization

The Data Division, which is one of the required divisions in
a program, is subdivided into sections. These are the File, Working-Storage, Linkage, and Communication Sections.

The File Section defines the structure of data files. Each file
is defined by a file description entry and one or more record
descriptions. Record descriptions are written immediately following the file description entry.

The Working-Storage Section describes records which are not part of external data files but are developed and processed internally. It also describes data items whose values are assigned in the source program and do not change during the execution of the object program.

The Linkage Section appears in the called program and describes data items that are to be referred to by the calling program and the called program. Its structure is the same as the Working-Storage Section.

The Communication Section describes the data item in the source program that will serve as the interface between the MCS and the program.

5.6.2.2 Data Division Structure

The following gives the general format of the sections in the Data Division, and defines the order of their presentation in the source program.

DATA DIVISION.

[FILE SECTION.

[file-description-entry [record-description-entry] . . .
sort-merge-file-description-entry

{ record-description-entry} . . .] . . .]

[WORKING-STORAGE SECTION.

[record-description-entry] . . .]

[LINKAGE SECTION.

[record-description-entry] . . .]

[COMMUNICATION SECTION.

[communication-description-entry] . . .]

5.7 Procedure Division

5.7.1 GENERAL DESCRIPTION

The Procedure Division must be included in every COBOL source program. This division contains nondeclarative procedures.

5.7.1.1 Procedures

A procedure is composed of a paragraph, or group of successive paragraphs, or a section, or a group of successive sections within the Procedure Division. If one paragraph is in a section, then all paragraphs must be in sections. A procedure-name is a word used to refer to a paragraph or section in the source program in which it occurs. It consists of a paragraph-name or a section-name.

The end of the Procedure Division and the physical end of the program is that physical position in a COBOL source program after which no further procedures appear.

A section consists of a section header followed by zero, one, or more successive paragraphs. A section ends immediately before the next section at the end of the Procedure Division.

A paragraph consists of a paragraph-name followed by a period and a space and by zero, one, or more successive sentences. A paragraph ends immediately before the next paragraph-name or section-name or at the end of the Procedure Division.

A sentence consists of one or more statements and is terminated by a period followed by a space.

A statement is a syntactically valid combination of words and symbols beginning with a COBOL verb.

The term 'identifier' is defined as the word or words necessary to make unique reference to a data item.

5.7.1.2 Execution

Execution begins with the first statement of the Procedure Division. Statements are then executed in the order in which they are presented for compilation, except where the rules indicate some other order.

5.7.1.3 Procedure Division Structure

5.7.1.3.1 PROCEDURE DIVISION HEADER

The Procedure Division is identified by and must begin with the following header:

PROCEDURE DIVISION [USING data-name-1 [, data-name-2] . . .].

5.7.1.3.2 PROCEDURE DIVISION BODY

The body of the Procedure Division must conform to one of the following formats:

Format 1

{section-name SECTION. [segment-number].

[paragraph-name. [sentence] . . .] . . . } . . .

Format 2

{paragraph-name. [sentence] . . . } . . .

5.7.2 STATEMENTS AND SENTENCES

There are three types of statements: conditional statements, compiler directing sentences, and imperative statements.

There are three types of sentences: conditional statements, compiler directing sentences, and imperative sentences.

5.7.2.1 Conditional Statements and Conditional Sentences

5.7.2.1.1 DEFINITION OF CONDITIONAL STATEMENT

A conditional statement specifies that the truth value of a condition is to be determined and that the subsequent action of the object program is dependent on this truth value.

A conditional statement is one of the following:

1. An IF, READ, or RETURN statement.
2. A DELETE, REWRITE, or WRITE statement that specifies the INVALID KEY phrase.
3. A RECEIVE statement that specifies a NO DATA phrase.

5.7.2.1.2 DEFINITION OF CONDITIONAL SENTENCE

A conditional sentence is a conditional statement, optionally preceded by an imperative statement, terminated by a period followed by a space.

5.7.2.2 Compiler Directing Statements and Compiler Directing Sentences

5.7.2.2.1 DEFINITION OF COMPILER DIRECTING STATEMENT

A compiler directing statement consists of a compiler directing verb and its operands. The compiler directing verb is COPY (see page 278, The COPY Statement). A compiler directing statement causes the compiler to take a specific action during compilation.

5.7.2.2.2 DEFINITION OF COMPILER DIRECTING SENTENCE

A compiler directing sentence is a single compiler directing statement terminated by a period followed by a space.

5.7.2.3 Imperative Statements and Imperative Sentences

5.7.2.3.1 DEFINITION OF IMPERATIVE STATEMENT

An imperative statement indicates a specific unconditional action to be taken by the object program. An imperative statement is any statement that is neither a conditional statement, nor a compiler directing statement. An imperative statement may consist of a sequence of imperative statements, each possibly separated from the next by a separator. The imperative verbs are:

ACCEPT	EXIT PROGRAM	RELEASE
ADD	GO	REWRITE (1)
CALL	MOVE	SEND
CLOSE	MULTIPLY	SORT
DELETE (1)	OPEN	STOP
DISPLAY	PERFORM	SUBTRACT
DIVIDE	RECEIVE (2)	WRITE (1)

(1) Without the optional INVALID KEY phrase
(2) Without the optional NO DATA phrase

When 'imperative-statement' appears in the general format of statements, 'imperative-statement' refers to that sequence of consecutive imperative statements that must be ended by a period or an ELSE phrase associated with a previous IF statement.

5.7.2.3.2 DEFINITION OF IMPERATIVE SENTENCE

An imperative sentence is an imperative statement terminated by a period followed by a space.

5.7.2.4 Categories of Statements

Category	Verbs
Arithmetic	ADD DIVIDE MULTIPLY SUBTRACT
Compiler Directing	{ COPY
Conditional	DELETE (INVALID KEY) IF READ RECEIVE (NO DATA) RETURN REWRITE (INVALID KEY) WRITE (INVALID KEY)
Data Movement	ACCEPT MESSAGE COUNT MOVE
Ending	{ STOP

Input-Output	ACCEPT CLOSE DELETE DISPLAY OPEN RECEIVE REWRITE SEND WRITE
Inter-Program Communicating	CALL
Ordering	RELEASE SORT
Procedure Branching	CALL EXIT PROGRAM GO TO PERFORM

IF is a verb in the COBOL sense; it is recognized that it is not a verb in English.

5.7.2.4.1 SPECIFIC STATEMENT FORMATS

The specific statement formats, together with a detailed discussion of the restrictions and limitations associated with each, appear in alphabetic sequence in the appropriate section of this document.

5.8 Reference Format

5.8.1 GENERAL DESCRIPTION

The reference format, which provides a standard method for describing COBOL source programs, is described in terms of character positions in a line on an input-output medium. Each implementor must define what is meant by lines and character positions for each input-output medium used with his compiler. Within these definitions, each COBOL compiler accepts source programs written in reference format and produces an output listing of the source program input in reference format.

The rules for spacing given in the discussion of the reference format take precedence over all other rules for spacing.

The divisions of a source program must be ordered as follows: the Identification Division, then the Environment Division, then the Data Division, then the Procedure Division. Each division must be written according to the rules for the reference format.

5.8.2 REFERENCE FORMAT REPRESENTATION

The reference format for a line is represented as follows:

```
|            |   |        |              |
Margin      Margin Margin  Margin         Margin
L              C A         B                   R
|            |   |    1  1 | 1  1              |
| 1  2  3  4  5  6 | 7 | 8  9  0  1 | 2  3  ... |
```

Sequence Number Area | Area A   Area B
                  Indicator Area

Margin L is immediately to the left of the leftmost character position of a line.

Margin C is between the 6th and 7th character positions of a line.

Margin A is between the 7th and 8th character positions of a line.

Margin B is between the 11th and 12th character positions of a line.

Margin R is immediately to the right of the rightmost character position of a line.

The sequence number area occupies six character positions (1–6), and is between margin L and margin C.

The indicator area is the 7th character position of a line.

Area A occupies character positions 8, 9, 10, and 11, and is between margin A and margin B.

Area B occupies a finite number of character positions specified by the implementor; it begins immediately to the right of margin B and terminates immediately to the left of margin R.

5.8.2.1 Sequence Numbers

A sequence number, consisting of six digits in the sequence area, may be used to label a source program line.

5.8.2.2 Continuation of Lines

Whenever a sentence, entry, phrase, or clause requires more than one line, it may be continued by starting subsequent line(s) in area B. These subsequent lines are called the continuation line(s). The line being continued is called the continued line. Any nonnumeric literal may be broken in such a way that part of it appears on a continuation line. A COBOL word and a numeric literal cannot be broken in such a way that part of it appears on a continuation line.

When the continued line contains a nonnumeric literal without closing quotation mark, a hyphen must appear in the indicator area on the continuation line, the first nonblank character in area B on the continuation line must be a quotation mark, and the continuation starts with the character immediately after that quotation mark. All spaces at the end of the continued line are considered part of the literal. Area A of a continuation line must be blank.

If there is no hyphen in the indicator area of a line, it is assumed that the last character in the preceding line is followed by a space.

5.8.2.3 Blank Lines

A blank line is one that is blank from margin C to margin R, inclusive. A blank line can appear anywhere in the source program, except immediately preceding a continuation line. (See paragraph 5.8.2.2 above.)

5.8.3 DIVISION, SECTION, PARAGRAPH FORMATS

5.8.3.1 Division Header

The division header must start in area A.

5.8.3.2 Section Header

The section header must start in area A.

A section consists of paragraphs in the Environment and Procedure Divisions and Data Division entries in the Data Division.

5.8.3.3 Paragraph Header, Paragraph-Name and Paragraph

A paragraph consists of a paragraph-name followed by a period and a space and by zero, one or more sentences, or a paragraph header followed by one or more entries. Comment lines may be included within a paragraph as indicated in paragraph 5.8.6. The paragraph header or paragraph-name starts in area A of any line following the first line of a division or a section.

The first sentence or entry in a paragraph begins either on the same line as the paragraph header or paragraph-name or in area B of the next nonblank line that is not a comment line. Successive sentences or entries either begin in area B of the same line as the preceding sentence or entry or in area B of the next nonblank line that is not a comment line.

When the sentences or entries of a paragraph require more than one line they may be continued as described in paragraph 5.8.2.2

5.8.4 DATA DIVISION ENTRIES

Each Data Division entry begins with a level indicator or a level-number, followed by a space, followed by its associated name, followed by a sequence of independent descriptive clauses. Each clause, except the last clause of an entry, may be terminated by either the separator semicolon or the separator comma. The last clause is always terminated by a period followed by a space. There are two types of Data Division entries: those which begin with a level indicator and those which begin with a level-number.

A level indicator is any of the following: FD, SD, CD. In those Data Division entries that begin with a level indicator, the level indicator begins in area A followed by a space and followed in area B with its associated name and appropriate descriptive information.

Those Data Division entries that begin with level-numbers are called data description entries.

A level-number has a value taken from the set of values 1 through 10. Level-numbers in the range 1 through 9 are written as a zero followed by a significant digit. At least one space must separate a level-number from the word following the level-number.

In those data description entries that begin with a level-number 01, the level-number begins in area A followed by a space and followed in area B by its associated record-name or item-name and appropriate descriptive information.

Successive data description entries may have the same format as the first or may be indented according to level-number. The entries in the output listing need be indented only if the input is indented. Indentation does not affect the magnitude of a level-number.

When level-numbers are to be indented, each new level-number may begin any number of spaces to the right of margin A. The extent of indentation to the right is determined only by the width of the physical medium.

5.8.5 COMMENT LINES

A comment line is any line with an asterisk in the continuation indicator area of the line. A comment line can appear as any line in a source program after the Identification Division header. Any combination of characters from the computer's character set may be included in area A and area B of that line. The asterisk and the characters in area A and area B will be produced on the listing but serve as documentation only. A special form of comment line represented by a stroke in the indicator area of the line causes page ejection prior to printing the comment.

Successive comment lines are allowed. Continuation of comment lines is permitted, except that each continuation line must contain an '*' in the indicator area.

5.9 Reserved Words

The following is a list of reserved words:

ACCEPT	CORRESPONDING	EXTEND	LESS
ACCESS	COUNT		LIMIT
ADD	CURRENCY	FD	LIMITS
ADVANCING		FILE	LINAGE
AFTER	DATA	FILE-CONTROL	LINAGE-COUNTER
ALL	DATE	FILLER	LINE
ALPHABETIC	DATE-COMPILED	FINAL	LINE-COUNTER
ALSO	DATE-WRITTEN	FIRST	LINES
ALTER	DAY	FOOTING	LINKAGE
ALTERNATE	DE	FOR	LOCK
AND	DEBUG-CONTENTS	FROM	LOW-VALUE
ARE	DEBUG-ITEM		LOW-VALUES
AREA	DEBUG-LINE	GENERATE	
AREAS	DEBUG-NAME	GIVING	MEMORY
ASCENDING	DEBUG-SUB-1	GO	MERGE
ASSIGN	DEBUG-SUB-2	GREATER	MESSAGE
AT	DEBUG-SUB-3	GROUP	MODE
AUTHOR	DEBUGGING		MODULES
	DECIMAL-POINT	HEADING	MOVE
BEFORE	DECLARATIVES	HIGH-VALUE	MULTIPLE
BLANK	DELETE	HIGH-VALUES	MULTIPLY
BLOCK	DELIMITED		
BOTTOM	DELIMITER	I-O	NATIVE
BY	DEPENDING	I-O-CONTROL	NEGATIVE
	DESCENDING	IDENTIFICATION	NEXT
CALL	DESTINATION	IF	NO
CANCEL	DETAIL	IN	NOT
CD	DISABLE	INDEX	NUMBER
CF	DISPLAY	INDEXED	NUMERIC
CH	DIVIDE	INDICATE	

CHARACTER	DIVISION	INITIAL	OBJECT-COMPUTER
CHARACTERS	DOWN	INITIATE	OCCURS
CLOCK-UNITS	DUPLICATES	INPUT	OF
CLOSE	DYNAMIC	INPUT-OUTPUT	OFF
COBOL		INSPECT	OMITTED
CODE	EGI	INSTALLATION	ON
CODE-SET	ELSE	INTO	OPEN
COLLATING	EMI	INVALID	OPTIONAL
COLUMN	ENABLE	IS	OR
COMMA	END		ORGANIZATION
COMMUNICATION	END-OF-PAGE	JUST	OUTPUT
COMP	ENTER	JUSTIFIED	OVERFLOW
COMPUTATIONAL	ENVIRONMENT		
COMPUTE	EOP	KEY	PAGE
CONFIGURATION	EQUAL		PAGE-COUNTER
CONTAINS	ERROR	LABEL	PERFORM
CONTROL	ESI	LAST	PF
CONTROLS	EVERY	LEADING	PH
COPY	EXCEPTION	LEFT	PIC
CORR	EXIT	LENGTH	PICTURE
PLUS	RERUN	SPACE	TYPE
POINTER	RESERVE	SPACES	
POSITION	RESET	SPECIAL-NAMES	UNIT
POSITIVE	RETURN	STANDARD	UNSTRING
PRINTING	REVERSED	STANDARD-1	UNTIL
PROCEDURE	REWIND	START	UP
PROCEDURES	REWRITE	STATUS	UPON
PROCEED	RF	STOP	USAGE
PROGRAM	RH	STRING	USE
PROGRAM-ID	RIGHT	SUB-QUEUE-1	USING
	ROUNDED	SUB-QUEUE-2	
QUEUE	RUN	SUB-QUEUE-3	VALUE
QUOTE		SUBTRACT	VALUES
QUOTES	SAME	SUM	VARYING
	SD	SUPPRESS	
RANDOM	SEARCH	SYMBOLIC	WHEN
RD	SECTION	SYNC	WITH
READ	SECURITY	SYNCHRONIZED	WORDS
RECEIVE	SEGMENT		WORKING-STORAGE
RECORD	SEGMENT-LIMIT	TABLE	WRITE
RECORDS	SELECT	TALLYING	
REDEFINES	SEND	TAPE	ZERO
REEL	SENTENCE	TERMINAL	ZEROES
REFERENCES	SEPARATE	TERMINATE	ZEROS

RELATIVE	SEQUENCE	TEXT	
RELEASE	SEQUENTIAL	THAN	+
REMAINDER	SET	THROUGH	−
REMOVAL	SIGN	THRU	•
RENAMES	SIZE	TIME	/
REPLACING	SORT	TIMES	••
REPORT	SORT-MERGE	TO	>
REPORTING	SOURCE	TOP	<
REPORTS	SOURCE-COMPUTER	TRAILING	=

6

COMPOSITE LANGUAGE SKELETON

6.1 General Description

This chapter contains the composite language skeleton of the American National Standard Minimum COBOL. It is intended to display complete and syntactically correct formats.

The leftmost margin on pages 104–107 is equivalent to margin A in a COBOL source program. The first indentation after the leftmost margin is equivalent to margin B in a COBOL source program. (See paragraph 5.8.2, for description of margin A and margin B.)

On pages 108–110 the leftmost margin indicates the beginning of the format for a new COBOL verb. The first indentation after the leftmost margin indicates continuation of the format of the COBOL verb.

Below is a summary of the formats shown on the following pages.

General format for Identification and Environment Divisions.

General formats for File Control Entry

General format for DATA Division

General format for Data Description Entry

General formats for Communication Description Entry

General formats for Procedure Division

General format for verbs

Miscellaneous general formats

General Format for Identification and Environment Divisions

IDENTIFICATION DIVISION.
PROGRAM-ID. program-name.

ENVIRONMENT DIVISION.
CONFIGURATION SECTION.
SOURCE-COMPUTER. computer-name [WITH DEBUGGING MODE].
OBJECT-COMPUTER. computer-name.
[SPECIAL-NAMES.
    [CURRENCY SIGN IS literal]
    [, DECIMAL-POINT IS COMMA].]
[INPUT-OUTPUT SECTION.
FILE-CONTROL.
    {file-control-entry} . . .]

General Formats for File Control Entry

FORMAT 1:
SELECT file-name
    ASSIGN TO implementor-name
    [; ORGANIZATION IS SEQUENTIAL]
    [; ACCESS MODE IS SEQUENTIAL]
    [; FILE STATUS IS data-name].

General Formats for File Control Entry (cont.)

FORMAT 2:

SELECT file-name

 ASSIGN TO implementor-name

 ; ORGANIZATION IS RELATIVE

  $\left[\; \text{; ACCESS MODE IS} \left\{ \begin{array}{l} \underline{\text{SEQUENTIAL}} \; [, \; \underline{\text{RELATIVE}} \; \text{KEY IS data-name-1}] \\ \underline{\text{RANDOM}}, \; \underline{\text{RELATIVE}} \; \text{KEY IS data-name-1} \end{array} \right\} \right]$

  [; FILE STATUS IS data-name-2].

FORMAT 3:

SELECT file-name

 ASSIGN TO implementor-name

 ; ORGANIZATION IS INDEXED

  $\left[\; \text{; ACCESS MODE IS} \left\{ \begin{array}{l} \underline{\text{SEQUENTIAL}} \\ \underline{\text{RANDOM}} \end{array} \right\} \right]$

  ; RECORD KEY IS data-name-1

  [; FILE STATUS IS data-name-2].

FORMAT 4:

SELECT file-name ASSIGN TO implementor-name.

General Format for Data Division

DATA DIVISION.
[FILE SECTION.
[FD file-name

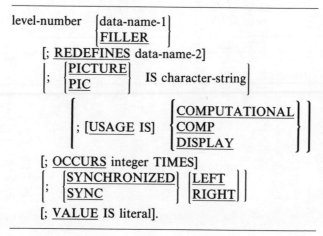

     | ; BLOCK CONTAINS integer { RECORDS / CHARACTERS } |

     ; LABEL RECORDS ARE [STANDARD / OMITTED]

       [; VALUE OF implementor-name IS literal].
[record-description-entry] . . .] . . .

[SD file-name.
{record-description-entry} . . .]

[WORKING-STORAGE SECTION.
[record-description-entry] . . .]

[LINKAGE SECTION.
[record-description-entry] . . .]

[COMMUNICATION SECTION.
[communication-description-entry] . . .]

General Format for Data Description Entry

---

level-number   [data-name-1 / FILLER]
     [; REDEFINES data-name-2]
   | ; {PICTURE / PIC} IS character-string |

       | ; [USAGE IS] {COMPUTATIONAL / COMP / DISPLAY} |

     [; OCCURS integer TIMES]
   | ; {SYNCHRONIZED / SYNC} [LEFT / RIGHT] |
     [; VALUE IS literal].

General Formats for Communication Description Entry

FORMAT 1:
CD cd-name; FOR INPUT
    [; SYMBOLIC QUEUE IS data-name-1]
    [; MESSAGE DATE IS data-name-2]
    [; MESSAGE TIME IS data-name-3]
    [; SYMBOLIC SOURCE IS data-name-4]
    [; TEXT LENGTH IS data-name-5]
    [; END KEY IS data-name-6]
    [; STATUS KEY IS data-name-7]
    [; MESSAGE COUNT IS data-name-8].

FORMAT 2:
CD cd-name; FOR OUTPUT
    [; DESTINATION COUNT IS data-name-1]
    [; TEXT LENGTH IS data-name-2]
    [; STATUS KEY IS data-name-3]
    [; ERROR KEY IS data-name-4]
    [; SYMBOLIC DESTINATION IS data-name-5].

General Formats for Procedure Division

FORMAT 1:
PROCEDURE DIVISION [USING data-name-1 [, data-name-2] . . .].
{section-name SECTION [segment-number].
[paragraph-name. [sentence] . . .] . . . } . . .

FORMAT 2:
PROCEDURE DIVISION [USING data-name-1 [, data-name-2] . . .].
{paragraph-name. [sentence] . . . } . . .

General Format for Verbs

ACCEPT identifier

ACCEPT cd-name MESSAGE COUNT

ADD $\begin{Bmatrix} \text{identifier-1} \\ \text{literal-1} \end{Bmatrix}$ TO identifier-2 [ROUNDED]

ADD $\begin{Bmatrix} \text{identifier-1} \\ \text{literal-1} \end{Bmatrix}$, $\begin{Bmatrix} \text{identifier-2} \\ \text{literal-2} \end{Bmatrix}$ ... GIVING identifier-3 [ROUNDED]

CALL literal [USING data-name-1 [, data-name-2] ...]

CLOSE file-name

DELETE file-name RECORD [; INVALID KEY imperative-statement]

DISPLAY $\begin{Bmatrix} \text{identifier} \\ \text{literal} \end{Bmatrix}$

DIVIDE $\begin{Bmatrix} \text{identifier-1} \\ \text{literal-1} \end{Bmatrix}$ BY $\begin{Bmatrix} \text{identifier-2} \\ \text{literal-2} \end{Bmatrix}$ GIVING identifier-3 [ROUNDED]

EXIT PROGRAM.

GO TO procedure-name

GO TO procedure-name-1 [, procedure-name-2] ..., procedure-name-n DEPENDING ON identifier

IF condition; imperative-statement-1 [; ELSE imperative-statement-2]

MOVE $\begin{Bmatrix} \text{identifier-1} \\ \text{literal} \end{Bmatrix}$ TO identifier-2

MULTIPLY $\begin{Bmatrix} \text{identifier-1} \\ \text{literal-1} \end{Bmatrix}$ BY $\begin{Bmatrix} \text{identifier-2} \\ \text{literal-2} \end{Bmatrix}$ GIVING identifier-3 [ROUNDED]

General Format for Verbs (cont.)

$$\underline{\text{OPEN}} \left\{ \begin{array}{l} \underline{\text{INPUT}}\ \text{file-name-1} \\ \underline{\text{OUTPUT}}\ \text{file-name-2} \\ \underline{\text{I-O}}\ \text{file-name-3} \end{array} \right\}$$

$$\underline{\text{PERFORM}}\ \text{procedure-name-1}\ \left[\begin{array}{l} \underline{\text{THROUGH}} \\ \underline{\text{THRU}} \end{array} \right]\ \text{procedure-name-2}$$

$$\underline{\text{PERFORM}}\ \text{procedure-name-1}\ \left[\begin{array}{l} \underline{\text{THROUGH}} \\ \underline{\text{THRU}} \end{array} \right]\ \text{procedure-name-2}\ \left\{ \begin{array}{l} \text{identifier-1} \\ \text{integer-1} \end{array} \right\}\ \underline{\text{TIMES}}$$

$$\underline{\text{PERFORM}}\ \text{procedure-name-1}\ \left[\begin{array}{l} \underline{\text{THROUGH}} \\ \underline{\text{THRU}} \end{array} \right]\ \text{procedure-name-2}\ \underline{\text{UNTIL}}\ \text{condition-1}$$

$\underline{\text{READ}}$ file-name RECORD; AT $\underline{\text{END}}$ imperative-statement

$\underline{\text{READ}}$ file-name RECORD; $\underline{\text{INVALID}}$ $\underline{\text{KEY}}$ imperative-statement

$\underline{\text{RECEIVE}}$ cd-name $\underline{\text{MESSAGE}}$ $\underline{\text{INTO}}$ identifier [; $\underline{\text{NO}}$ $\underline{\text{DATA}}$ imperative-statement]

$\underline{\text{RELEASE}}$ record-name

$\underline{\text{RETURN}}$ file-name RECORD; AT $\underline{\text{END}}$ imperative-statement

$\underline{\text{REWRITE}}$ record-name

$\underline{\text{REWRITE}}$ record-name; $\underline{\text{INVALID}}$ $\underline{\text{KEY}}$ imperative-statement

$\underline{\text{REWRITE}}$ record-name [; $\underline{\text{INVALID}}$ $\underline{\text{KEY}}$ imperative-statement]

$$\underline{\text{SEND}}\ \text{cd-name}\ [\underline{\text{FROM}}\ \text{identifier-1}]\ \left[\begin{array}{l} \underline{\text{WITH}}\ \underline{\text{EMI}} \\ \underline{\text{WITH}}\ \underline{\text{EGI}} \end{array} \right]$$

$$\left[\left\{ \begin{array}{l} \underline{\text{BEFORE}} \\ \underline{\text{AFTER}} \end{array} \right\}\ \underline{\text{ADVANCING}}\ \left\{ \begin{array}{l} \text{identifier-2} \\ \text{integer} \\ \underline{\text{PAGE}} \end{array} \right\} \right]$$

109

General Format for Verbs (cont.)

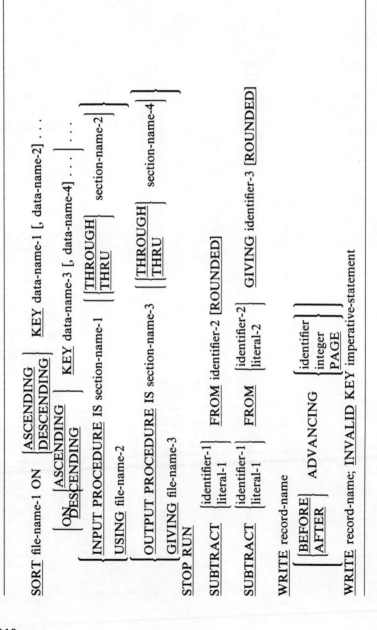

SORT file-name-1 ON $\left\{ \begin{matrix} \underline{\text{ASCENDING}} \\ \underline{\text{DESCENDING}} \end{matrix} \right\}$ KEY data-name-1 [, data-name-2] . . .

$\left[\text{ON} \left\{ \begin{matrix} \underline{\text{ASCENDING}} \\ \underline{\text{DESCENDING}} \end{matrix} \right\} \text{KEY data-name-3 [, data-name-4]} \right] \dots$ . . .

$\left\{ \begin{matrix} \underline{\text{INPUT PROCEDURE}} \text{ IS section-name-1} \left[\left\{ \begin{matrix} \underline{\text{THROUGH}} \\ \underline{\text{THRU}} \end{matrix} \right\} \text{section-name-2} \right] \\ \underline{\text{USING}} \text{ file-name-2} \end{matrix} \right\}$

$\left\{ \begin{matrix} \underline{\text{OUTPUT PROCEDURE}} \text{ IS section-name-3} \left[\left\{ \begin{matrix} \underline{\text{THROUGH}} \\ \underline{\text{THRU}} \end{matrix} \right\} \text{section-name-4} \right] \\ \underline{\text{GIVING}} \text{ file-name-3} \end{matrix} \right\}$

STOP RUN

SUBTRACT $\left\{ \begin{matrix} \text{identifier-1} \\ \text{literal-1} \end{matrix} \right\}$ FROM identifier-2 [ROUNDED]

SUBTRACT $\left\{ \begin{matrix} \text{identifier-1} \\ \text{literal-1} \end{matrix} \right\}$ FROM $\left\{ \begin{matrix} \text{identifier-2} \\ \text{literal-2} \end{matrix} \right\}$ GIVING identifier-3 [ROUNDED]

WRITE record-name

$\left[\left\{ \begin{matrix} \underline{\text{BEFORE}} \\ \underline{\text{AFTER}} \end{matrix} \right\} \text{ADVANCING} \left\{ \begin{matrix} \text{identifier} \\ \text{integer} \\ \underline{\text{PAGE}} \end{matrix} \right\} \right]$

WRITE record-name; INVALID KEY imperative-statement

Miscellaneous General Formats

RELATION CONDITION:

$$\begin{Bmatrix} \text{identifier-1} \\ \text{literal-1} \end{Bmatrix} \begin{Bmatrix} \text{IS [NOT] GREATER THAN} \\ \text{IS [NOT] LESS THAN} \\ \text{IS [NOT] EQUAL TO} \\ \text{IS [NOT]} > \\ \text{IS [NOT]} < \\ \text{IS [NOT]} = \end{Bmatrix} \begin{Bmatrix} \text{identifier-2} \\ \text{literal-2} \end{Bmatrix}$$

CLASS CONDITION:

$$\text{identifier IS [NOT]} \begin{Bmatrix} \text{NUMERIC} \\ \text{ALPHABETIC} \end{Bmatrix}$$

SIGN CONDITION:

$$\text{identifier IS [NOT]} \begin{Bmatrix} \text{POSITIVE} \\ \text{NEGATIVE} \\ \text{ZERO} \end{Bmatrix}$$

IDENTIFIER:
data-name [(subscript)]

COPY:
COPY text-name

SECTION II

Nucleus

1

INTRODUCTION TO THE NUCLEUS

1.1 Function

The Nucleus in American National Standard Minimum COBOL provides a basic language capability for the internal processing of data within the basic structure of the four divisions of a program.

1.2 Restriction on Overall Language in American National Standard Minimum COBOL

The separators, comma and semicolon, are included.

All data-names must begin with an alphabetic character. Qualification is not included, therefore, all data-names and paragraph-names must be unique.

Only the figurative constants ZERO, ZEROS, ZEROES, SPACE, and SPACES are permitted.

A word or numeric literal cannot be broken in such a way that part of it appears on a continuation line.

A level-number must have a value of 01 through 10 and must be written as two digits.

A user-defined word is composed of not more than 15 characters.

A system-name is composed of not more than 15 characters.

2

IDENTIFICATION DIVISION IN THE NUCLEUS

2.1 General Description

The Identification Division must be included in every COBOL source program. This division identifies the source program and the resultant output listing.

2.2 Organization

Paragraph headers identify the type of information contained in the paragraph. The name of the program must be given in the PROGRAM-ID paragraph.

2.2.1 STRUCTURE

The following is the general format of the paragraph in the Identification Division and it defines the order of presentation in the source program. Paragraph 2.3 defines the PROGRAM-ID paragraph.

2.2.1.1 General Format

IDENTIFICATION DIVISION.
PROGRAM-ID. program-name.

2.2.1.2 Syntax Rules

(1) The Identification Division must begin with the reserved words IDENTIFICATION DIVISION followed by a period and a space.

2.3 The PROGRAM-ID Paragraph

2.3.1 FUNCTION

The PROGRAM-ID paragraph gives the name by which a program is identified.

2.3.2 GENERAL FORMAT

PROGRAM-ID. program-name.

2.3.3 SYNTAX RULES

(1) The program-name must conform to the rules for formation of a user-defined word.

2.3.4 GENERAL RULES

(1) The PROGRAM-ID paragraph must contain the name of the program and must be present in every program.

(2) The program-name identifies the source program and all listings pertaining to a particular program.

3

ENVIRONMENT DIVISION IN THE NUCLEUS

3.1 Configuration Section

3.1.1 THE SOURCE-COMPUTER PARAGRAPH

3.1.1.1 Function

The SOURCE-COMPUTER paragraph identifies the computer upon which the program is to be compiled.

3.1.1.2 General Format

SOURCE-COMPUTER. computer-name.

3.1.1.3 Syntax Rules

(1) Computer-name is a system-name.

3.1.1.4 General Rules

(1) Fixed computer-names are assigned by the individual implementor.

(2) The computer-name may provide a means for identifying equipment configuration, in which case the computer-name and its implied configuration are specified by each implementor.

3.1.2 THE OBJECT-COMPUTER PARAGRAPH

3.1.2.1 Function

The OBJECT-COMPUTER paragraph identifies the computer on which the program is to be executed.

3.1.2.2 General Format

OBJECT-COMPUTER. computer-name.

3.1.2.3 Syntax Rules

(1) Computer-name is a system-name.

3.1.2.4 General Rules

(1) The computer-name may provide a means for identifying equipment configuration, in which case the computer-name and its implied configuration are specified by each implementor.

3.1.3 THE SPECIAL-NAMES PARAGRAPH

3.1.3.1 Function

The SPECIAL-NAMES paragraph provides a means of specifying the character to represent the currency symbol and of interchanging the function of the comma and period in the PICTURE character-string.

3.1.3.2 General Format

SPECIAL-NAMES.
    [CURRENCY SIGN IS literal]
    [, DECIMAL-POINT IS COMMA].

3.1.3.4 General Rules

(1) The literal which appears in the CURRENCY SIGN IS literal clause is used in the PICTURE CLAUSE TO REPRESENT THE CURRENCY SYMBOL. The literal is limited to a single character and must not be one of the following characters.

(a) digits 0 thru 9;

(b) alphabetic characters A, B, C, D, L, P, R, S, V, X, Z, or the space;

(c) special characters '*', '+', '−', ',', '.', ';', '(', ')', '"', '/', '='.

If this clause is not present, only the currency sign is used in the PICTURE clause.

(2)   The clause DECIMAL-POINT IS COMMA means that the function of comma and period are exchanged in the character-string of the PICTURE clause and in numeric literals.

4

DATA DIVISION IN THE NUCLEUS

4.1 Working-Storage Section

The Working-Storage Section is composed of the section header, followed by record description entries. Each Working-Storage Section record name and noncontiguous item name must be unique.

4.1.1 WORKING-STORAGE RECORDS

Data elements and constants in Working-Storage which bear a definite hierarchic relationship to one another must be grouped into records according to the rules for formation of record descriptions. All clauses which are used in record descriptions in the File Section can be used in record descriptions in the Working-Storage Section.

4.1.2 INITIAL VALUES

The initial value of any item in the Working-Storage Section is specified by using the VALUE clause with the data item.

4.2 The Data Description—Complete Entry Skeleton

4.2.1 FUNCTION

A data description entry specifies the characteristics of a particular item of data.

4.2.2 GENERAL FORMAT

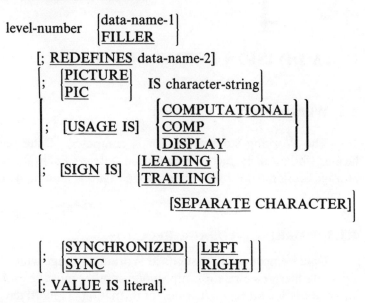

4.2.3 SYNTAX RULES

(1)   The level-number may be any number from 01–10.

(2)   The clauses may be written in any order with two exceptions: the data-name-1 or FILLER clause must immediately follow the level-number; the REDEFINES clause, when used, must immediately follow the data-name-1 clause.

(3)   The PICTURE clause must be specified for every elementary item.

4.2.4 GENERAL RULES

(1)   The clauses SYNCHRONIZED and PICTURE must not be specified except for an elementary data item.

4.3 The Data-Name or FILLER Clause

4.3.1 FUNCTION

A data-name specifies the name of the data being described. The word FILLER specifies an elementary item of the logical record that cannot be referred to explicitly.

4.3.2 GENERAL FORMAT

$$\begin{bmatrix} \text{data-name} \\ \underline{\text{FILLER}} \end{bmatrix}$$

4.3.3. SYNTAX RULES

(1) In the File, Working-Storage, and Linkage Sections, a data-name or the key word FILLER must be the first word following the level-number in each data description entry.

4.3.4 GENERAL RULES

(1) The key word FILLER may be used to name an elementary item in a record. Under no circumstances can a FILLER item be referred to explicitly.

4.4 Level-Number

4.4.1 FUNCTION

The level-number shows the hierarchy of data within a logical record. In addition, it is used to identify entries for working storage items and linkage items.

4.4.2 GENERAL FORMAT

level-number

4.4.3 SYNTAX RULES

(1) A level-number is required as the first element in each data description entry and must be written as two digits.

(2) Data description entries subordinate to an FD or SD entry must have level-numbers with the values 01 through 10. (See page 184 for FD and page 258 for SD.)

(3) Data description entries in the Working-Storage Section and Linkage Section must have level-numbers with the values 01 through 10.

4.4.4 GENERAL RULES

(1) The level-number 01 identifies the first entry in each record description.

(2) Multiple level 01 entries subordinate to any given level indicator represent implicit redefinitions of the same area.

4.5 The PICTURE Clause

4.5.1 FUNCTION

The PICTURE clause describes the general characteristics and editing requirements of an elementary item.

4.5.2 GENERAL FORMAT

$$\begin{bmatrix} \underline{PICTURE} \\ \underline{PIC} \end{bmatrix} \text{ IS character-string}$$

4.5.3 SYNTAX RULES

(1) A PICTURE clause can be specified only at the elementary item level.

(2) A character-string consists of certain allowable combinations of characters in the COBOL character set used as symbols.

The allowable combinations determine the category of the elementary item.

(3) The maximum number of characters allowed in the character-string is 30.

(4) The PICTURE clause must be specified for every elementary item.

(5) PIC is an abbreviation for PICTURE.

4.5.4 GENERAL RULES

(1) There are four categories of data that can be described with a PICTURE clause: numeric, alphanumeric, alphanumeric edited, and numeric edited.

(2) To define an item as numeric:

(a) Its PICTURE character-string can only contain the symbols '9', 'S', and 'V'. The number of digit positions that can be described by the PICTURE character-string must range from 1 to 18 inclusive; and

(b) If unsigned, its contents when represented in standard data format must be a combination of the Arabic numerals '0', '1', '2', '3', '4', '5', '6', '7', '8', and '9'; if signed, the item may also contain a '+', '−', or other representation of an operational sign.

(3) To define an item as alphanumeric:

(a) Its PICTURE character-string is restricted to certain combinations of the symbols 'X', '9', and the item is treated as if the character-string contained all 'X's. A PICTURE character-string which contains all 9's does not define an alphanumeric item; and

(b) Its contents when represented in standard data format are allowable characters in the computer's character set.

(4) To define an item as alphanumeric edited:

(a) Its PICTURE character-string is restricted to certain combinations of the following symbols: 'X', '9', and 'B'; and the character-string must contain at least one 'B' and at least one 'X'; and

(b) The contents when represented in standard data format are allowable characters in the computer's character set.

(5) To define an item as numeric edited:

(a) Its PICTURE character-string is restricted to certain combinations of the symbols 'B', 'V', 'Z', '9', ',', '.', '*', '+', '—', and the currency symbol. The allowable combinations are determined from the order of precedence of symbols and the editing rules; and

    1. The number of digit positions that can be represented in the PICTURE character-string must range from 1 to 18 inclusive; and

    2. The character-string must contain at least one 'B', 'Z', '*', '+', ',', '.', '—', or currency symbol.

(b) The contents of the character positions of these symbols that are allowed to represent a digit in standard data format, must be one of the numerals.

(6) The size of an elementary item, where size means the number of character positions occupied by the elementary item in standard data format, is determined by the number of allowable symbols that represent character positions. An integer which is enclosed in parentheses following the symbols ',', 'X', '9', 'Z', '*', 'B', '+', '—', or the currency symbol indicates the number of consecutive occurrences of the symbol. Note that the following symbols may appear only once in a given PICTURE: 'S', 'V', and '.'.

(7) The functions of the symbols used to describe an elementary item are explained as follows:

B Each 'B' in the character-string represents a character position into which the space character will be inserted.

S The letter 'S' is used in a character-string to indicate the presence, but neither the representation nor, necessarily, the position of an operational sign; it must be written as the leftmost character in the PICTURE. The 'S' is not counted in determining the size (in terms of standard data format characters) of the elementary item unless the entry is subject to a SIGN clause which specifies the optional SEPARATE CHARACTER phrase. (See paragraph 4.7, The SIGN Clause.)

V The 'V' is used in a character-string to indicate the location of the assumed decimal point and may only appear once in a character-string. The 'V' does not represent a character position and therefore is not counted in the size of the elementary item. When the assumed decimal point is to the right of the rightmost symbol in the string the 'V' is redundant.

X Each 'X' in the character-string is used to represent a character position which contains any allowable character from the computer's character set.

Z Each 'Z' in a character-string may only be used to represent the leftmost leading numeric character positions which will be replaced by a space character when the contents of that character position is zero. Each 'Z' is counted in the size of the item.

9 Each '9' in the character-string represents a character position which contains a numeral and is counted in the size of the item.

, Each ',' (comma) in the character-string represents a character position into which the character ',' will be inserted. This character position is counted in the size of the item. The insertion character ',' must not be the last character in the PICTURE character-string.

. When the character '.' (period) appears in the character-string it is an editing symbol which represents the decimal point for alignment purposes and in addition, represents a character position into which the character '.' will be inserted. The character '.' is counted in the size of the item. For a given program the functions of the period and comma are exchanged if the clause DECIMAL-POINT IS COMMA is stated in the SPECIAL-NAMES paragraph. In this exchange the rules for the period apply to the comma and the rules for the comma apply to the period wherever they appear in a PICTURE clause. The insertion character '.' must not be the last character in the PICTURE character-string.

+ and − These symbols are used as editing sign control symbols. When used, they represent the character position into which the editing sign control symbol will be placed. The symbols are mutually exclusive in any one character-string and each character used in the symbol is counted in determining the size of the data item.

* Each '*' (asterisk) in the character-string represents a leading numeric character position into which an asterisk will be placed when the contents of that position is zero. Each '*' is counted in the size of the item.

cs The currency symbol in the character-string represents a character position into which a currency symbol is to be placed. The currency symbol in a character-string is represented by either the currency sign or by the single character specified in the CURRENCY SIGN clause in the SPECIAL-NAMES paragraph. The currency symbol is counted in the size of the item.

4.5.5 EDITING RULES

(1)   There are two general methods of performing editing in the PICTURE clause, either by insertion or by suppression and replacement. There are four types of insertion editing available. They are:

(a) Simple insertion

(b) Special insertion

(c) Fixed insertion

(d) Floating insertion

There are two types of suppression and replacement editing:

(a) Zero suppression and replacement with spaces

(b) Zero suppression and replacement with asterisks

(2)   The type of editing which may be performed upon an item is dependent upon the category to which the item belongs. Table 1 specifies which type of editing may be performed upon a given category.

(3)   Floating insertion editing and editing by zero suppression and replacement are mutually exclusive in a PICTURE clause. Only one type of replacement may be used with zero suppression in a PICTURE clause.

(4)   Simple Insertion Editing. The ',' (comma) and 'B' (space) are used as insertion characters. The insertion characters are counted in the size of the item and represent the position in the item into which the character will be inserted.

(5)   Special Insertion Editing. The '.' (period) is used as the insertion character. In addition to being an insertion character it also represents the decimal point for alignment purposes. The insertion character used for the actual decimal point is counted in the size of the item. The use of the assumed decimal point, represented by the symbol 'V' and the actual decimal point, represented by the insertion character, in the same PICTURE character-string is disallowed. The result of special insertion editing is the appearance of the insertion character in the item in the same position as shown in the character-string.

(6)   Fixed Insertion Editing. The currency symbol and the editing sign control symbols, '+', '−', are the insertion characters. Only one currency symbol and only one of the editing sign control

Table 1

Category	Type of Editing
Numeric	None
Alphanumeric	None
Alphanumeric Edited	Simple insertion 'B'
Numeric Edited	All, subject to rules in rule 3

symbols can be used in a given PICTURE character-string. The symbol '+' or '−', when used, must be either the leftmost or rightmost character position to be counted in the size of the item. The currency symbol must be the leftmost character position to be counted in the size of the item except that it can be preceded by either a '+' or a '−' symbol. Fixed insertion editing results in the insertion character occupying the same character position in the edited item as it occupied in the PICTURE character-string. Editing sign control symbols produce the results as shown in Table 2 depending upon the value of the data item.

(7)   Floating Insertion Editing. The currency symbol and editing sign control symbol '+' or '−' are the floating insertion characters and as such are mutually exclusive in a given PICTURE character-string.

Floating insertion editing is indicated in a PICTURE character-string by using a string of at least two of the floating insertion characters. This string of floating insertion characters may contain any of the fixed insertion symbols or have fixed insertion characters immediately to the right of this string. These simple insertion characters are part of the floating string.

The leftmost character of the floating insertion string represents the leftmost limit of the floating symbol in the data item. The rightmost character of the floating string represents the rightmost limit of the floating symbols in the data item.

The second floating character from the left represents the leftmost limit of the numeric data that can be stored in the data

Table 2

Editing Symbol in Picture Character-String	Result	
	Data Item Positive Or Zero	Data Item Negative
+	+	−
−	space	−

item. Non-zero numeric data may replace all the characters at or to the right of this limit.

In a PICTURE character-string, there are only two ways of representing floating insertion editing. One way is to represent any or all of the leading numeric character positions on the left of the decimal point by the insertion character. The other way is to represent all of the numeric character positions in the PICTURE character-string by the insertion character.

If the insertion characters are only to the left of the decimal point in the PICTURE character-string, the result is that a single floating insertion character will be placed into the character position immediately preceding either the decimal point or the first non-zero digit in the data represented by the insertion symbol string, whichever is farther to the left in the PICTURE character-string. The character positions preceding the insertion character are replaced with spaces.

If all numeric character positions in the PICTURE character-string are represented by the insertion character, the result depends upon the value of the data. If the value is zero the entire data item will contain spaces. If the value is not zero, the result is the same as when the insertion character is only to the left of the decimal point.

To avoid truncation, the minimum size of the PICTURE character-string for the receiving data item must be the number of characters in the sending data item, plus the number of non-floating insertion characters being edited into the receiving data item, plus one for the floating insertion character.

(8) Zero Suppression Editing. The suppression of leading zeroes in numeric character positions is indicated by the use of the alphabetic character 'Z' or the character '*' (asterisk) as suppression symbols in a PICTURE character-string. These symbols are mutually exclusive in a given PICTURE character-string. Each suppression symbol is counted in determining the size of the item. If 'Z' is used the replacement character will be the space and if the asterisk is used, the replacement character will be '*'.

Zero suppression and replacement is indicated in a PIC-

TURE character-string by using a string of one or more of the allowable symbols to represent leading numeric character positions which are to be replaced when the associated character position in the data contains a zero. Any of the simple insertion characters embedded in the string of symbols or to the immediate right of this string are part of the string.

In a PICTURE character-string, there are only two ways of representing zero suppression. One way is to represent any or all of the leading numeric character positions to the left of the decimal point by suppression symbols. The other way is to represent all of the numeric character positions in the PICTURE character-string by suppression symbols.

If the suppression symbols appear only to the left of the decimal point, any leading zero in the data which corresponds to a symbol in the string is replaced by the replacement character. Suppression terminates at the first non-zero digit in the data represented by the suppression symbol string or at the decimal point, whichever is encountered first.

If all numeric character positions in the PICTURE character-string are represented by suppression symbols and the value of the data is not zero the result is the same as if the suppression characters were only to the left of the decimal point. If the value is zero and the suppression symbol is 'Z', the entire data item will be spaces. If the value is zero and the suppression symbol is '*', the data item will be all '*' except for the actual decimal point.

(9) The symbols '+', '−', '*', 'Z', and the currency symbol, when used as floating replacement characters, are mutually exclusive within a given character-string.

4.5.6 PRECEDENCE RULES

The chart following shows the order of precedence when using characters as symbols in a character-string. An 'X' at an intersection indicates that the symbol(s) at the top of the column may precede, in a given character-string, the symbol(s) at the left of the row. Arguments appearing in braces indicate that the symbols are mutually exclusive. The currency symbol is indicated by the symbol 'cs'.

132

PICTURE Character Precedence Chart

Second Symbol \ First Symbol	Non-Floating Insertion Symbols: B	,	.	{+/-}	{+/-}	cs	Floating Insertion Symbols: [Z/*]	[Z/*]	{+/-}	{+/-}	cs	cs	Other Symbols: 9	X	S	V
Non-Floating Insertion Symbols — B	x	x	x	x		x	x	x	x	x	x	x	x	x		x
,	x	x	x	x		x	x	x	x	x	x	x	x			x
.	x	x		x		x	x			x		x	x			
{+/-}																
{+/-}	x	x	x			x	x	x	x		x	x	x			x
cs				x												
Floating Insertion Symbols — [Z/*]	x	x		x			x	x								
[Z/*]	x	x	x	x			x	x	x							x
{+/-}	x	x					x			x						
{+/-}	x	x	x				x			x	x					x
cs	x	x		x							x					
cs	x	x	x	x							x	x				x
Other Symbols — 9	x	x	x	x			x	x		x		x		x	x	x
X	x													x	x	
S																
V	x	x		x			x	x		x		x		x		x

At least one of the symbols 'X', 'Z', '9', or '*', or at least two of the symbols '+', '−', or 'cs' must be present in a PICTURE character-string.

Non-floating insertion symbols '+' and '−', and the floating insertion symbols 'Z', '*', '+', '−', and 'cs' appear twice in the PICTURE character precedence chart on page 133. The leftmost column and uppermost row for each symbol represents its use to the left of the decimal point position. The second appearance of the symbol in the chart represents its use to the right of the decimal point position.

4.6 The REDEFINES Clause

4.6.1 FUNCTION

The REDEFINES clause allows the same computer storage area to be described by different data description entries.

4.6.2 GENERAL FORMAT

level-number data-name-1; <u>REDEFINES</u> data-name-2

Note: Level-number, data-name-1 and the semicolon are shown in the above format to improve clarity. Level-number and data-name-1 are not part of the REDE-FINES clause.

4.6.3 SYNTAX RULES

(1) The REDEFINES clause, when specified, must immediately follow data-name-1.

(2) The level-numbers of data-name-1 and data-name-2 must be identical.

(3) This clause must not be used in level 01 entries in the File Section.

(4) The data description entry for data-name-2 cannot contain a REDEFINES clause. Data-name-2 cannot be subordinate to an

entry which contains a REDEFINES clause. The data description entry for data-name-2 cannot contain an OCCURS clause.

(5)   No entry having a level-number numerically lower than the level-number of data-name-2 and data-name-1 may occur between the data description entries of data-name-2 and data-name-1.

4.6.4 GENERAL RULES

(1)   Redefinition starts at data-name-2 and ends when a level-number less than or equal to that of data-name-2 is encountered.

(2)   When the level-number of data-name-1 is other than 01, it must specify the same number of character positions that the data item referenced by data-name-2 contains. It is important to observe that the REDEFINES clause specifies the redefinition of a storage area, not of the data items occupying the area.

(3)   Multiple redefinitions of the same character positions are permitted. The entries giving the new descriptions of the character positions must follow the entries defining the area being redefined, without intervening entries that define new character positions. Multiple redefinitions of the same character positions must all use the data-name of the entry that originally defined the area.

(4)   The entries giving the new description of the character positions must not contain any VALUE clauses.

(5)   Multiple level 01 entries subordinate to any given level indicator represent implicit redefinitions of the same area.

4.7 The SIGN Clause

4.7.1 FUNCTION

The SIGN clause specifies the position and the mode of representation of the operational sign when it is necessary to describe these properties explicitly.

4.7.2 GENERAL FORMAT

[SIGN IS] $\begin{bmatrix} \text{LEADING} \\ \text{TRAILING} \end{bmatrix}$

[SEPARATE CHARACTER]

4.7.3 SYNTAX RULES

(1) The SIGN clause may be specified only for a numeric data description entry whose PICTURE contains the character 'S', or a group item containing at least one such numeric data description entry.

(2) The numeric data description entries to which the SIGN clause applies must be described as usage is DISPLAY.

(3) At most one SIGN clause may apply to any given numeric data description entry.

4.7.4 GENERAL RULES

(1) The optional SIGN clause, if present, specifies the position and the mode of representation of the operational sign for the numeric data description entry to which it applies, or for each numeric data description entry subordinate to the group to which it applies. The SIGN clause applies only to numeric data description entries whose PICTURE contains the character 'S'; the 'S' indicates the presence of, but neither the representation nor, necessarily, the position of the operational sign.

(2) A numeric data description entry whose PICTURE contains the character 'S', but to which no optional SIGN clause applies, has an operational sign, but neither the representation nor, necessarily, the position of the operational sign is specified by the character 'S'. In this (default) case, the implementor will define the position and representation of the operational sign. General rules 3 through 5 do not apply to such signed numeric data items.

(3) If the optional SEPARATE CHARACTER phrase is not present, then:

136

(a) The operational sign will be presumed to be associated with the leading (or, respectively, trailing) digit position of the elementary numeric data item.

(b) The letter 'S' in a PICTURE character-string is not counted in determining the size of the item (in terms of standard data format characters).

(c) The implementor defines what constitutes valid sign(s), for data items.

(4)   If the optional SEPARATE CHARACTER phrase is present, then:

(a) The operational sign will be presumed to be the leading (or, respectively, trailing) character position of the elementary numeric data item; this character position is not a digit position.

(b) The letter 'S' in a PICTURE character-string is counted in determining the size of the item (in terms of standard data format characters).

(c) The operational signs for positive and negative are the standard data format characters '+' and '−', respectively.

(5)   Every numeric data description entry whose PICTURE contains the character 'S' is a signed numeric data description entry. If a SIGN clause applies to such an entry and conversion is necessary for purposes of computation or comparisons, conversion takes place automatically.

4.8 The SYNCHRONIZED Clause

4.8.1 FUNCTION

The SYNCHRONIZED clause specifies the alignment of an elementary item on the natural boundaries of the computer memory (see page 83, Item Alignment for Increased Object-Code Efficiency).

4.8.2 GENERAL FORMAT

$$\left\{ \begin{array}{l} \text{SYNCHRONIZED} \\ \text{SYNC} \end{array} \right\} \left\{ \begin{array}{l} \text{LEFT} \\ \text{RIGHT} \end{array} \right\}$$

4.8.3 SYNTAX RULES

(1) This clause may only appear with an elementary item.

(2) SYNC is an abbreviation for SYNCHRONIZED.

4.8.4 GENERAL RULES

(1) This clause specifies that the subject data item is to be aligned in the computer such that no other data item occupies any of the character positions between the leftmost and rightmost natural boundaries delimiting this data item. If the number of character positions required to store this data item is less than the number of character positions between those natural boundaries, the unused character positions (or portions thereof) must not be used for any other data item. Such unused character positions, however, are included in:

(a) The size of any group item(s) to which the elementary item belongs; and

(b) The character positions redefined when this data item is the object of a REDEFINES clause.

(2) SYNCHRONIZED not followed by either RIGHT or LEFT specifies that the elementary item is to be positioned between natural boundaries in such a way as to effect efficient utilization of the elementary data item. The specific positioning is, however, determined by the implementor.

(3) SYNCHRONIZED LEFT specifies that the elementary item is to be positioned such that it will begin at the left character position of the natural boundary in which the elementary item is placed.

(4) SYNCHRONIZED RIGHT specifies that the elementary item is to be positioned such that it will terminate on the right

character position of the natural boundary in which the elementary item is placed.

(5) Whenever a SYNCHRONIZED item is referenced in the source program, the original size of the item, as shown in the PICTURE clause, is used in determining any action that depends on size, such as justification, truncation, or overflow.

(6) If the data description of an item contains the SYNCHRONIZED clause and an operational sign, the sign of the item appears in the normal operational sign position, regardless of whether the item is SYNCHRONIZED LEFT or SYNCHRONIZED RIGHT.

(7) When the SYNCHRONIZED clause is specified in a data description entry of a data item that also contains an OCCURS clause, or in a data description entry of a data item subordinate to a data description entry that contains an OCCURS clause, then:

(a) Each occurrence of the data item is SYNCHRONIZED.

(b) Any implicit FILLER generated for other data items within that same table are generated for each occurrence of those data items. (See general rule 8b.)

(8) This clause is hardware dependent and in addition to rules 1 through 7, the implementor must specify how elementary items associated with this clause are handled regarding:

(a) The formation on the external media of records or groups containing elementary items whose data description contains the SYNCHRONIZED clause.

(b) Any necessary generation of implicit FILLER, if the elementary item immediately preceding an item containing the SYNCHRONIZED clause does not terminate at an appropriate natural boundary. Such automatically generated FILLER positions are included in:

1. The size of any group to which the FILLER item belongs; and
2. The number of character positions allocated when the group item of which the FILLER item is a part appears as the object of a REDEFINES clause.

139

(9) An implementor may, at his option, specify automatic alignment for any internal data formats except, within a record, data items whose usage is DISPLAY. However, the record itself may be synchronized.

(10) Any rules for synchronization of the records of a data file, as this effects the synchronization of elementary items, will be specified by the implementor.

4.9 The USAGE Clause

4.9.1 FUNCTION

The USAGE clause specifies the format of a data item in the computer storage.

4.9.2 GENERAL FORMAT

$$[\underline{USAGE} \text{ IS}] \left\{ \begin{array}{l} \underline{COMPUTATIONAL} \\ \underline{COMP} \\ \underline{DISPLAY} \end{array} \right\}$$

4.9.3 SYNTAX RULES

(1) The PICTURE character-string of a COMPUTATIONAL item can contain only '9's, the operational sign character 'S', the implied decimal point character 'V'. (See paragraph 4.5, The PICTURE Clause.)

(2) COMP is an abbreviation for COMPUTATIONAL.

4.9.4 GENERAL RULES

(1) The USAGE clause can be written at any level. If the USAGE clause is written at a group level, it applies to each elementary item in the group. The USAGE clause of an elementary item cannot contradict the USAGE clause of a group to which the item belongs.

(2) This clause specifies the manner in which a data item is represented in the storage of a computer. It does not affect the use of the data item, although the specifications for some statements in the Procedure Division may restrict the USAGE clause of the operands referred to. The USAGE clause may affect the radix or type of character representation of the item.

(3) A COMPUTATIONAL item is capable of representing a value to be used in computations and must be numeric. If a group item is described as COMPUTATIONAL, the elementary items in the group are COMPUTATIONAL. The group item itself is not COMPUTATIONAL (cannot be used in computations).

(4) The USAGE IS DISPLAY clause indicates that the format of the data is a standard data format.

(5) If the USAGE clause is not specified for an elementary item, or for any group to which the item belongs, the usage is implicitly DISPLAY.

4.10 The VALUE Clause

4.10.1 FUNCTION

The VALUE clause defines the value of constants and the initial value of working storage items.

4.10.2 GENERAL FORMAT

VALUE IS literal

4.10.3 SYNTAX RULES

(1) A signed numeric literal must have associated with it a signed numeric PICTURE character-string.

(2) All numeric literals in a VALUE clause of an item must have a value which is within the range of values indicated by the PIC-TURE clause, and must not have a value which would require truncation of nonzero digits. Nonnumeric literals in a VALUE

141

clause of an item must not exceed the size indicated by the PIC-TURE clause.

4.10.4 GENERAL RULES

(1)   The VALUE clause must not conflict with other clauses in the data description of the item or in the data description within the hierarchy of the item. The following rules apply:

(a) If the category of the item is numeric, the literal in the VALUE clause must be numeric. If the literal defines the value of a working storage item, the literal is aligned in the data item according to the standard alignment rules. (See page 82, Standard Alignment Rules.)

(b) If the category of the item is alphanumeric, alphanumeric edited or numeric edited, the literal in the VALUE clause must be a nonnumeric literal. The literal is aligned in the data item as if the data item had been described as alphanumeric. (See Standard Alignment Rules.) Editing characters in the PICTURE clause are included in determining the size of the data item (see paragraph 4.5, The PICTURE Clause) but have no effect on initialization of the data item. There-fore, the VALUE for an edited item is presented in an edited form.

(2)   A figurative constant may be substituted where a literal is specified.

(3)   Rules governing the use of the VALUE clause differ with the respective sections of the Data Division:

(a) The VALUE clause cannot be used in the File Section.

(b) In the Working-Storage Section, the VALUE clause may be used to specify the initial value of any data item; in which case the clause causes the item to assume the specified value at the start of the object program. If the VALUE clause is not used in an item's description, the initial value is un-defined.

(c) The VALUE clause cannot be used in the Linkage Sec-tion.

(3)   The VALUE clause must not be stated in a data description entry that contains an OCCURS clause, or in an entry that is subordinate to an entry containing an OCCURS clause. (See page 170, The OCCURS Clause.)

(4)   The VALUE clause must not be stated in a data description entry that contains a REDEFINES clause, or in an entry that is subordinate to an entry containing a REDEFINES clause.

(5)   If the VALUE clause is used in an entry at the group level, the literal must be a nonnumeric literal, and the group area is initialized without consideration for the individual elementary or group items contained within this group. The VALUE clause cannot be stated at the subordinate levels within this group.

(6)   The VALUE clause must not be written for a group containing items with descriptions including SYNCHRONIZED or USAGE (other than USAGE IS DISPLAY).

5

PROCEDURE DIVISION IN THE NUCLEUS

5.1 Conditional Expressions

Conditional expressions identify conditions that are tested to enable the object program to select between alternate paths of control depending upon the truth value of the condition. Conditional expressions are specified in the IF and PERFORM statements. There is one category of conditions associated with conditional expressions: Simple condition.

5.1.1 SIMPLE CONDITION

The simple conditions are the relation and class conditions. A simple condition has a truth value of 'true' or 'false'.

5.1.1.1 Relation Condition

A relation condition causes a comparison of two operands, each of which may be the data item referenced by an identifier or a literal. A relation condition has a truth value of 'true' if the relation exists between the operands. Comparison of two numeric operands is permitted regardless of the formats specified in their respective USAGE clauses. However, for all other comparisons the operands must have the same usage. If either of the operands is a group item, the nonnumeric comparison rules apply.

The general format of a relation condition is as follows:

$$
\begin{Bmatrix} \text{identifier-1} \\ \text{literal-1} \end{Bmatrix}
\begin{Bmatrix}
\text{IS [NOT] \underline{GREATER} THAN} \\
\text{IS [NOT] \underline{LESS} THAN} \\
\text{IS [NOT] \underline{EQUAL} TO} \\
\text{IS [NOT] >} \\
\text{IS [NOT] <} \\
\text{IS [NOT] =}
\end{Bmatrix}
\begin{Bmatrix} \text{identifier-2} \\ \text{literal-2} \end{Bmatrix}
$$

NOTE: The required relational characters '>', '<', and '=' are not underlined to avoid confusion with other symbols such as '≥' (greater than or equal to).

The first operand (identifier-1 or literal-1) is called the subject of the condition; the second operand (identifier-2 or literal-2) is called the object of the condition. The relation condition must contain at least one reference to a variable.

The relational operator specifies the type of comparison to be made in a relation condition. A space must precede and follow each reserved word comprising the relational operator. When used, 'NOT' and the next key word or relation character are one relational operator that defines the comparison to be executed for truth value; e.g., 'NOT EQUAL' is a truth test for an 'unequal' comparison; 'NOT GREATER' is a truth test for an 'equal' or 'less' comparison. The meaning of the relational operators is as follows:

Meaning	Relational Operator
Greater than or not greater than	IS [NOT] GREATER THAN IS [NOT] >
Less than or not less than	IS [NOT] LESS THAN IS [NOT] <
Equal to or not equal to	IS [NOT] EQUAL TO IS [NOT] =

Note: The required relational characters '>', '<', and '=' are not underlined to avoid confusion with other symbols such as '≥' (greater than or equal to).

5.1.1.1.1 COMPARISON OF NUMERIC OPERANDS

For operands whose class is numeric (see Section I, paragraph 5.3.3.3), a comparison is made with respect to the algebraic value of the operands. The length of the literal, in terms of number of digits represented, is not significant. Zero is considered a unique value regardless of the sign.

Comparison of these operands is permitted regardless of the manner in which their usage is described. Unsigned numeric operands are considered positive for purposes of comparison.

145

5.1.1.1.2 COMPARISON OF NONNUMERIC OPERANDS

For nonnumeric operands, or one numeric and one nonnumeric operand, a comparison is made with respect to the computer's native collating sequence of characters. If one of the operands is specified as numeric, it must be an integer data item or an integer literal and:

1. If the nonnumeric operand is an elementary data item or a nonnumeric literal, the numeric operand is treated as though it were moved to an elementary alphanumeric data item of the same size as the numeric data item (in terms of standard data format characters), and the contents of this alphanumeric data item were then compared to the nonnumeric operand. (See paragraph 5.9, The MOVE Statement.)

2. If the nonnumeric operand is a group item, the numeric operand is treated as though it were moved to a group item of the same size as the numeric data item (in terms of standard data format characters), and the contents of this group item were then compared to the nonnumeric operand. (See paragraph 5.9, The MOVE Statement.)

3. A non-integer numeric operand cannot be compared to a nonnumeric operand.

The size of an operand is the total number of standard data format characters in the operand. Numeric and nonnumeric operands may be compared only when their usage is the same.

There are two cases to consider: operands of equal size and operands of unequal size.

1. Operands of equal size. If the operands are of equal size, comparison effectively proceeds by comparing characters in corresponding character positions starting from the high order end and continuing until either a pair of unequal characters is encountered or the low order end of the operand is reached, whichever comes first. The operands are determined to be equal if all pairs of characters com-

pare equally through the last pair, when the low order end is reached.

The first encountered pair of unequal characters is compared to determine their relative position in the collating sequence. The operand that contains the character that is positioned higher in the collating sequence is considered to be the greater operand.

2. Operands of unequal size. If the operands are of unequal size, comparison proceeds as though the shorter operand were extended on the right by sufficient spaces to make the operands of equal size.

5.1.2 CLASS CONDITION

The class condition determines whether the operand is numeric, that is, consists entirely of the characters '0', '1', '2', '3', . . ., '9', with or without the operational sign, or alphabetic, that is, consists entirely of the characters 'A', 'B', 'C', . . ., 'Z', space. The general format for the class condition is as follows:

identifier IS [NOT] $\begin{Bmatrix} \text{NUMERIC} \\ \text{ALPHABETIC} \end{Bmatrix}$

The usage of the operand being tested must be described as display. When used, 'NOT' and the next key word specify one class condition that defines the class test to be executed for truth value; e.g., 'NOT NUMERIC' is a truth test for determining that an operand is nonnumeric.

The NUMERIC test cannot be used with an item whose data description describes the item as alphabetic or as a group item composed of elementary items whose data description indicates the presence of operational sign(s). If the data description of the item being tested does not indicate the presence of an operational sign, the item being tested is determined to be numeric only if the contents are numeric and an operational sign is not present. If the data description of the item does indicate the presence of an operational sign, the item being tested is determined to be numeric only if the contents are numeric and a valid operational sign is present. Valid operational signs for data items described with the

SIGN IS SEPARATE clause are the standard data format characters, '+', and '−'; the implementor defines what constitutes valid sign(s) for data items not described with the SIGN IS SEPARATE clause.

The ALPHABETIC text cannot be used with an item whose data description describes the item as numeric. The item being tested is determined to be alphabetic only if the contents consist of any combination of the alphabetic characters 'A' through 'Z' and the space.

5.2 Common Phrases and General Rules for Statement Formats

In the statement descriptions that follow, one phrase appears frequently: the ROUNDED phrase.

In the discussion below, a resultant-identifier is that identifier associated with a result of an arithmetic operation.

5.2.1 THE ROUNDED PHRASE

If, after decimal point alignment, the number of places in the fraction of the result of an arithmetic operation is greater than the number of places provided for the fraction of the resultant-identifier, truncation is relative to the size provided for the resultant-identifier. When rounding is requested, the absolute value of the resultant-identifier is increased by one (1) whenever the most significant digit of the excess is greater than or equal to five (5).

5.2.2 THE ARITHMETIC STATEMENTS

The arithmetic statements are the ADD, DIVIDE, MULTIPLY, and SUBTRACT statements. They have several common features.

1. The data descriptions of the operands need not be the same; any necessary conversion and decimal point alignment is supplied throughout the calculation.

2. The maximum size of each operand is eighteen (18) decimal digits. The composite of operands, which is a hypothetical data item resulting from the superimposition of specified operands in a statement aligned on their decimal points (see paragraph 5.4, The ADD Statement, and paragraph 5.13, the SUBTRACT Statement) must not contain more than eighteen decimal digits.

5.2.3 OVERLAPPING OPERANDS

When a sending and receiving item in an arithmetic statement or a MOVE statement share a part of their storage areas, the result of the execution of such a statement is undefined.

5.2.4 INCOMPATIBLE DATA

Except for the class condition (see paragraph 5.1.2, The Class Condition), when the contents of a data item are referenced in the Procedure Division and the contents of that data item are not compatible with the class specified for that data item by its PICTURE clause, then the result of such a reference is undefined.

5.3 The ACCEPT Statement

5.3.1 FUNCTION

The ACCEPT statement causes low volume data to be made available to the specified data item.

5.3.2 GENERAL FORMAT

ACCEPT identifier

5.3.3 GENERAL RULES

(1)   The ACCEPT statement causes the transfer of data from the hardware device. This data replaces the contents of the data item named by the identifier.

149

(2)   The implementor will define the size of a data transfer for the hardware device.

(3)   If a hardware device is capable of transferring data of the same size as the receiving data item, the transferred data is stored in the receiving data item.

(4)   If a hardware device is not capable of transferring data of the same size as the receiving data item, then:

(a) If the size of the receiving data item exceeds the size of the transferred data, the transferred data is stored aligned to the left in the receiving data item. Only one transfer of data is provided.

(b) If the size of the transferred data exceeds the size of the receiving data item, only the leftmost characters of the transferred data are stored in the receiving data item. The remaining characters of the transferred data which do not fit into the receiving data item are ignored.

(5)   The device that the implementor specifies as standard is used.

5.4 The ADD Statement

5.4.1 FUNCTION

The ADD statement causes two numeric operands to be summed and the result to be stored.

5.4.2 GENERAL FORMAT

Format 1

$$\underline{ADD} \quad \begin{Bmatrix} \text{identifier-1} \\ \text{literal-1} \end{Bmatrix} \quad \underline{TO} \text{ identifier-2 } \underline{[ROUNDED]}$$

Format 2

$$\underline{ADD} \quad \begin{Bmatrix} \text{identifier-1} \\ \text{literal-1} \end{Bmatrix} \text{ , } \begin{Bmatrix} \text{identifier-2} \\ \text{literal-2} \end{Bmatrix}$$

$$\underline{GIVING} \text{ identifier-3 } \underline{[ROUNDED]}$$

5.4.3 SYNTAX RULES

(1)   Each identifier must refer to an elementary numeric item, except that in Format 2 the identifier following the word GIVING must refer to either an elementary numeric item or an elementary numeric edited item.

(2)   Each literal must be a numeric literal.

(3)   The composite of operands must not contain more than 18 digits (see paragraph 5.2.2, The Arithmetic Statements.)

(a) In Format 1 the composite of operands is determined by using both of the operands in a given statement.

(b) In Format 2 the composite of operands is determined by using all of the operands in a given statement excluding identifier-3.

5.4.4 GENERAL RULES

(1)   See paragraph 5.2.1, The ROUNDED Phrase; paragraph 5.2.2, The Arithmetic Statements; and paragraph 5.2.3, Overlapping Operands.

(2)   If Format 1 is used, the value of identifier-1 or literal-1 is added to the current value of identifier-2 storing the result immediately into identifier-2.

(3)   If Format 2 is used, the values of the operands preceding the word GIVING are added together, then the sum is stored as the new value of identifier-3, the resultant-identifier.

(4)   The compiler insures that enough places are carried so as not to lose any significant digits during execution.

5.5 The DISPLAY Statement

5.5.1 FUNCTION

The DISPLAY statement causes low volume data to be transferred to an appropriate hardware device.

5.5.2 GENERAL FORMAT

$$\underline{\text{DISPLAY}} \quad \begin{bmatrix} \text{identifier} \\ \text{literal} \end{bmatrix}$$

5.5.3 SYNTAX RULES

(1) The literal may be any figurative constant.

(2) If the literal is numeric, then it must be an unsigned integer.

5.5.4 GENERAL RULES

(1) The DISPLAY statement causes the contents of the operand to be transferred to the hardware device in the order listed.

(2) The implementor will define, for each hardware device, the size of a data transfer for the hardware device.

(3) If a figurative constant is specified as the operand, only a single occurrence of the figurative constant is displayed.

(4) If the hardware device is capable of receiving data of the same size as the data item being transferred, then the data item is transferred.

(5) If the hardware device is not capable of receiving data of the same size as the data item being transferred, then one of the following applies:

(a) If the size of the data item being transferred exceeds the size of the data that the hardware device is capable of receiving in a single transfer, the data beginning with the leftmost character is stored aligned to the left in the receiving hardware device. Only one transfer of data is provided.

(b) If the size of the data item that the hardware device is capable of receiving exceeds the size of the data being transferred, the transferred data is stored aligned to the left in the receiving hardware device.

(6) The implementor's standard display device is used.

5.6 The DIVIDE Statement

5.6.1 FUNCTION

The DIVIDE statement divides one numeric data item by another and sets the value of a data item equal to the quotient.

5.6.2 GENERAL FORMAT

$$\underline{\text{DIVIDE}} \quad \begin{Bmatrix} \text{identifier-1} \\ \text{literal-1} \end{Bmatrix} \quad \underline{\text{BY}} \quad \begin{Bmatrix} \text{identifier-2} \\ \text{literal-2} \end{Bmatrix}$$

$$\underline{\text{GIVING}} \text{ identifier-3 } [\underline{\text{ROUNDED}}]$$

5.6.3 SYNTAX RULES

(1) Each identifier must refer to an elementary numeric item, except that any identifier associated with the GIVING phrase must refer to either an elementary numeric item or an elementary numeric edited item.

(2) Each literal must be a numeric literal.

5.6.4 GENERAL RULES

(1) See paragraph 5.2.1, The ROUNDED Phrase; paragraph 5.2.2, The Arithmetic Statements; and paragraph 5.2.3, Overlapping Operands for a description of these functions.

(2) The value of identifier-1 or literal-1 is divided by the value of identifier-2 or literal-2 and the result is stored in identifier-3.

5.7 The GO TO Statement

5.7.1 FUNCTION

The GO TO statement causes control to be transferred from one part of the Procedure Division to another.

153

5.7.2 GENERAL FORMAT

Format 1

<u>GO</u> TO procedure-name-1

Format 2

<u>GO</u> TO procedure-name-1 [, procedure-name-2] . . . ,

procedure-name-n <u>DEPENDING</u> ON identifier

5.7.3 SYNTAX RULES

(1)   Identifier is the name of a numeric elementary item described without any positions to the right of the assumed decimal point.

(2)   If a GO TO statement, represented by Format 1 appears in a consecutive sequence of imperative statements within a sentence, it must appear as the last statement in that sequence.

5.7.4 GENERAL RULES

(1)   When a GO TO statement, represented by Format 1 is executed, control is transferred to procedure-name-1.

(2)   When a GO TO statement represented by Format 2 is executed, control is transferred to procedure-name-1, procedure-name-2, etc., depending on the value of the identifier being 1, 2, . . ., n. If the value of the identifier is anything other than the positive or unsigned integers 1, 2, . . ., n, then no transfer occurs and control passes to the next statement in the normal sequence for execution.

5.8 The IF Statement

5.8.1 FUNCTION

The IF statement causes a condition (see page 144, Conditional Expressions) to be evaluated. The subsequent action of the subject program depends on whether the value of the condition is true or false.

5.8.2 GENERAL FORMAT

IF condition; imperative-statement-1 [; ELSE imperative-statement-2]

5.8.3 SYNTAX RULES

(1) Imperative-statement-1 and imperative-statement-2 represent one or more imperative statements.

5.8.4 GENERAL RULES

(1) When an IF statement is executed, the following transfers of control occur:

(a) If the condition is true, imperative-statement-1 is executed. If imperative-statement-1 contains a procedure branching statement, control is explicitly transferred in accordance with the rules of that statement. (See page 94, Categories of Statements.) If imperative-statement-1 does not contain a procedure branching statement, the ELSE phrase, if specified, is ignored and control passes to the next executable sentence.

(b) If the condition is false, imperative-statement-1 is ignored, and imperative-statement-2, if specified, is executed. If imperative-statement-1 contains a procedure branching statement, control is explicitly transferred in accordance with the rules of that statement. (See page 94, Categories of Statements.) If imperative-statement-2 does not contain a procedure branching statement, control passes to the next executable sentence. If the ELSE imperative-statement-2 phrase is not specified, imperative-statement-1 is ignored and control passes to the next executable sentence.

5.9 The MOVE Statement

5.9.1 FUNCTION

The MOVE statement transfers data, in accordance with the rules of editing, to one data area.

5.9.2 GENERAL FORMAT

$$\underline{\text{MOVE}} \quad \begin{Bmatrix} \text{identifier-1} \\ \text{literal} \end{Bmatrix} \quad \underline{\text{TO}} \ \text{identifier-2}$$

5.9.3 SYNTAX RULES

(1)   Identifier-1 and literal represent the sending area; identifier-2 represents the receiving area.

5.9.4 GENERAL RULES

(1)   The data designated by the literal or identifier-1 is moved to identifier-2. Any subscripting associated with identifier-2 is evaluated immediately before the data is moved to the respective data item.

(2)   Any MOVE in which the sending and receiving items are both elementary items is an elementary move. Every elementary item belongs to one of the following categories: numeric, alphanumeric, numeric edited, alphanumeric edited. These categories are described in the PICTURE clause. Numeric literals belong to the category numeric, and nonnumeric literals belong to the category alphanumeric.

   The following rules apply to an elementary move between these categories:

   (a) A numeric edited or alphanumeric edited data item must not be moved to a numeric or numeric edited data item.

   (b) A non-integer numeric literal or a non-integer numeric data item must not be moved to an alphanumeric or alphanumeric edited data item.

   (c) All other elementary moves are legal and are performed according to the rules given in general rule 3.

(3)   Any necessary conversion of data from one form of internal representation to another takes place during legal elementary moves, along with any editing specified for the receiving data item:

   (a) When an alphanumeric edited or alphanumeric item is a receiving item alignment and any necessary space filling takes place as defined under Standard Alignment Rules on page 82. If the size of the sending item is greater than the size of the receiving item, the excess characters are truncated on the right after the receiving item is filled. If the sending item is described as being signed numeric, the operational sign will not be moved; if the operational sign occupied a separate character position (see paragraph 4.7, The SIGN Clause), that character will not be moved and the size of the sending item will be considered to be one less than its actual size (in terms of standard data format characters).

(b) When a numeric or numeric edited item is the receiving item, alignment by decimal point and any necessary zero-filling takes place as defined under the Standard Alignment Rules on page 82, except where zeroes are replaced because of editing requirements.

1. When a signed numeric item is the receiving item, the sign of the sending item is placed in the receiving item. (See paragraph 4.7, The SIGN Clause). Conversion of the representation of the sign takes place as necessary. If the sending item is unsigned, a positive sign is generated for the receiving item.

2. When an unsigned numeric item is the receiving item, the absolute value of the sending item is moved and no operational sign is generated for the receiving item.

3. When a data item described as alphanumeric is the sending item, data is moved as if the sending item were described as an unsigned numeric integer.

(4)   Any move that is not an elementary move is treated exactly as if it were an alphanumeric to alphanumeric elementary move, except that there is no conversion of data from one form of internal representation to another. In such a move, the receiving area will be filled without consideration for the individual elementary or group items contained within either the sending or receiving area.

(5) Data in Table 3 summarizes the legality of the various types of MOVE statements. The general rule reference indicates the rule that prohibits the move or the behavior of a legal move.

5.10 The MULTIPLY Statement

5.10.1 FUNCTION

The MULTIPLY statement causes numeric data items to be multiplied and sets the value of a data item equal to the result.

5.10.2 GENERAL FORMAT

$$\underline{\text{MULTIPLY}} \quad \begin{bmatrix} \text{identifier-1} \\ \text{literal-1} \end{bmatrix} \quad \underline{\text{BY}} \quad \begin{bmatrix} \text{identifier-2} \\ \text{literal-2} \end{bmatrix}$$

$$\underline{\text{GIVING}} \text{ identifier-3 } [\underline{\text{ROUNDED}}]$$

Table 3

Category of Sending Data Item	Category of Receiving Data Item	
	Alphanumeric Edited Alphanumeric	Numeric Integer Numeric Non-Integer Numeric Edited
ALPHANUMERIC	Yes/3a	Yes/3b
ALPHANUMERIC EDITED	Yes/3a	No/2b
NUMERIC INTEGER	Yes/3a	Yes/3b
NUMERIC NON-INTEGER	No/2c	Yes/3b
NUMERIC EDITED	Yes/3a	No/2a

5.10.3 SYNTAX RULES

(1) Each identifier must refer to a numeric elementary item, except that identifier-3 following the word GIVING must refer to either an elementary numeric item or an elementary numeric edited item.

(2) Each literal must be a numeric literal.

5.10.4 GENERAL RULES

(1) See paragraph 5.2.1, The ROUNDED Phrase; paragraph 5.2.2, The Arithmetic Statements; paragraph 5.2.3, Overlapping Operands.

(2) The value of identifier-1 or literal-1 is multiplied by identifier-2 or literal-2 and the result is stored in identifier-3.

5.11 The PERFORM Statement

5.11.1 FUNCTION

The PERFORM statement is used to transfer control explicitly to one or more procedures and to return control implicitly whenever execution of the specified procedure is complete.

5.11.2 GENERAL FORMAT

Format 1

PERFORM procedure-name-1 $\left\{ \begin{matrix} \text{THROUGH} \\ \text{THRU} \end{matrix} \right\}$

procedure-name-2 $\Big]$

Format 2

PERFORM procedure-name-1 $\left\{\left[\begin{matrix} \underline{\text{THROUGH}} \\ \underline{\text{THRU}} \end{matrix}\right]\right.$

procedure-name-2$\left.\right]$ $\left\{\begin{matrix} \text{identifier-1} \\ \text{integer-1} \end{matrix}\right\}$ $\underline{\text{TIMES}}$

Format 3

PERFORM procedure-name-1 $\left\{\left[\begin{matrix} \underline{\text{THROUGH}} \\ \underline{\text{THRU}} \end{matrix}\right]\right.$

procedure-name-2$\left.\right]$ $\underline{\text{UNTIL}}$ condition-1

5.11.3 SYNTAX RULES

(1) Each identifier represents a numeric elementary item described in the Data Division. In Format 2, identifier-1 must be described as a numeric integer.

(2) The words THRU and THROUGH are equivalent.

(3) Condition-1 may be any conditional expression as described in paragraph 5.1, Conditional Expressions.

5.11.4 GENERAL RULES

(1) When the PERFORM statement is executed, control is transferred to the first statement of the procedure named procedure-name-1 (except as indicated in general rule 4b). This transfer of control occurs only once for each execution of a PERFORM statement. For those cases where a transfer of control to the named procedure does take place, an implicit transfer of control to the next executable statement following the PERFORM statement is established as follows:

(a) If procedure-name-1 is a paragraph-name and procedure-name-2 is not specified, then the return is after the last statement of procedure-name-1.

160

(b) If procedure-name-1 is a section-name and procedure-name-2 is not specified, then the return is after the last statement of the last paragraph in procedure-name-1.

(c) If procedure-name-2 is specified and it is a paragraph-name, then the return is after the last statement of the paragraph.

(d) If procedure-name-2 is specified and it is a section-name, then the return is after the last statement of the last paragraph in the section.

(2)   There is no necessary relationship between procedure-name-1 and procedure-name-2 except that a consecutive sequence of operations is to be executed beginning at the procedure named procedure-name-1 and ending with the execution of the procedure named procedure-name-2. In particular, GO TO and PERFORM statements may occur between procedure-name-1 and the end of procedure-name-2. If there are two or more logical paths to the return point, then procedure-name-2 may be the name of a paragraph consisting of no statements, to which all of these paths must lead.

(3)   If control passes to these procedures by means other than a PERFORM statement, control will pass through the last statement of the procedure to the next executable statement as if no PERFORM statement mentioned these procedures.

(4)   The PERFORM statements operate as follows with rule 3 above applying to all formats:

(a) Format 1 is the basic PERFORM statement. A procedure referenced by this type of PERFORM statement is executed once and then control passes to the next executable statement following the PERFORM statement.

(b) Format 2 is the PERFORM . . . TIMES. The procedures are performed the number of times specified by integer-1 or by the initial value of the data item referenced by identifier-1 for that execution. If, at the time of execution of a PER-FORM statement, the value of the data item referenced by identifier-1 is equal to zero or is negative, control passes to the next executable statement following the PERFORM statement. Following the execution of the procedures the specified number of times, control is transferred to the next executable statement following the PERFORM statement.

During execution of the PERFORM statement, references to identifier-1 cannot alter the number of times the procedures are to be executed from that which was indicated by the initial value of identifier-1.

(c) Format 3 is the PERFORM . . . UNTIL. The specified procedures are performed until the condition specified by the UNTIL phrase is true. When the condition is true, control is transferred to the next executable statement after the PERFORM statement. If the condition is true when the PERFORM statement is entered, no transfer to procedure-name-1 takes place, and control is passed to the next executable statement following the PERFORM statement.

(5) If a sequence of statements referred to by a PERFORM statement includes another PERFORM statement, the sequence of procedures associated with the included PERFORM must itself either be totally included in, or totally excluded from the logical sequence referred to by the first PERFORM. Thus, an active PERFORM statement, whose execution point begins within the range of another active PERFORM statement, must not allow control to pass to the exit of the other active PERFORM statement; furthermore, two or more such active PERFORM statements may not have a common exit. See the illustration below.

```
x PERFORM a THRU m     x PERFORM a THRU m
a ────────────────┐    a ──────────────────┐
d PERFORM f THRU j │    d PERFORM f THRU j   │
f ──────────┐      │    h                    │
j ──────────┘      │    m ───────────────────┘
m ─────────────────┘    f ──────────┐
                        j ──────────┘
```

x PERFORM a THRU m

a ──────────────────┐
f ──────────┐   │
m ──────────┼───┐   │
j ──────────┘   │   │
                └───┘

d PERFORM f THRU j

(6) A PERFORM statement that appears in a section that is not in an independent segment can have within its range only one of the following:

(a) Sections and/or paragraphs wholly contained in one or more non-independent segments.

(b) Sections and/or paragraphs wholly contained in a single independent segment.

(7) A PERFORM statement that appears in an independent segment can have within its range only one of the following:

(a) Sections and/or paragraphs wholly contained in one or more non-independent segments.

(b) Sections and/or paragraphs wholly contained in the same independent segment as that PERFORM statement.

5.12 The STOP Statement

5.12.1 FUNCTION

The STOP statement causes a permanent suspension of the execution of the object program.

5.12.2 GENERAL FORMAT

STOP RUN

5.12.3 SYNTAX RULES

(1) If a STOP RUN statement appears in a consecutive sequence of imperative statements within a sentence, it must appear as the last statement in that sequence.

5.12.4 GENERAL RULES

(1) The RUN phrase causes the ending procedure established by the installation and/or the compiler is instituted.

5.13 The SUBTRACT Statement

5.13.1 FUNCTION

The SUBTRACT statement is used to subtract one numeric data item from one item, and set the value of another item equal to the results.

5.13.2 GENERAL FORMAT

Format 1

SUBTRACT $\begin{bmatrix} \text{identifier-1} \\ \text{literal-1} \end{bmatrix}$

FROM identifier-2 [ROUNDED]

Format 2

SUBTRACT $\begin{bmatrix} \text{identifier-1} \\ \text{literal-1} \end{bmatrix}$

FROM $\begin{bmatrix} \text{identifier-2} \\ \text{literal-2} \end{bmatrix}$

GIVING identifier-3 [ROUNDED]

5.13.3 SYNTAX RULES

(1) Each identifier must refer to a numeric elementary item except that in Format 2, the identifier following the word GIVING must refer to either an elementary numeric item or an elementary numeric edited item.

(2) Each literal must be a numeric literal.

(3) The composite of operands must not contain more than 18 digits. (See paragraph 5.2.2, The Arithmetic Statements.)

(a) In Format 1 the composite of operands is determined by using both of the operands in a given statement.

(b) In Format 2 the composite of operands is determined by using all of the operands in a given statement excluding identifier-3.

5.13.4 GENERAL RULES

(1) See paragraph 5.2.1, The ROUNDED Phrase; paragraph 5.2.3, Overlapping Operands.

(2) In Format 1, the value of identifier-1 or literal-1 is subtracted from the current value of identifier-2 storing the result immediately into identifier-2.

(3) In Format 2, the value of identifier-1 or literal-1 is subtracted from the value of identifier-2 or literal-2 and the result of the subtraction is stored as the new value of identifier-3.

(4) The compiler insures enough places are carried so as not to lose significant digits during execution.

Table Handling Module

1

INTRODUCTION TO THE TABLE HANDLING MODULE

1.1 Function

The Table Handling module in American National Standard Minimum COBOL provides a capability for defining tables of contiguous data items and accessing an item relative to its position in the table. Language facility is provided for specifying how many times an item is to be repeated. Each item may be identified through use of a subscript (see page 83). The capability is provided for accessing items in a one-dimensional fixed length table.

2

DATA DIVISION IN THE TABLE HANDLING MODULE

2.1 The OCCURS Clause

2.1.1 FUNCTION

The OCCURS clause eliminates the need for separate entries for repeated data items and supplies information required for the application of subscripts.

2.1.2 GENERAL FORMAT

OCCURS integer TIMES

2.1.3 SYNTAX RULES

(1)   The OCCURS clause cannot be specified in a data description entry that has an 01 level-number.

2.1.4 GENERAL RULES

(1)   The OCCURS clause is used in defining tables and other homogeneous sets of repeated data items. Whenever the OCCURS clause is used, the data-name which is the subject of this entry must be subscripted whenever it is referred to in a statement. Further, if the subject of this entry is the name of a group item, then all data-names belonging to the group must be subscripted whenever they are used as operands, except as the object of a REDEFINES clause. (See Section I, paragraph 5.3.3.8.1, Subscripting, paragraph 5.3.3.8.2, Identifier.)

(2)   Except for the OCCURS clause itself, all data description clauses associated with an item whose description includes an

OCCURS clause apply to each occurrence of the item described. (See restriction in general rule 3 on page 143.)

(3) The number of occurrences of the subject entry is defined as follows:

(a) The value of integer represents the exact number of occurrences.

SECTION IV

Sequential I-O Module

1

INTRODUCTION TO THE SEQUENTIAL I-O MODULE

1.1 Function

The Sequential I-O module in American National Standard Minimum COBOL provides a capability to access records of a file in established sequence. The sequence is established as a result of writing the records to the file.

1.2 Language Concepts

1.2.1 ORGANIZATION

Sequential files are organized such that each record in the file except the first has a unique predecessor record, and each record except the last has a unique successor record. These predecessor-successor relationships are established by the order of WRITE statements when the file is created. Once established, the predecessor-successor relationships do not change except in the case where records are added to the end of the file.

1.2.2 ACCESS MODE

In the sequential access mode, the sequence in which records are accessed is the order in which the records were originally written.

1.2.3 CURRENT RECORD POINTER

The current record pointer is a conceptual entity used in this document to facilitate specification of the next record to be accessed within a given file. The concept of the current record pointer has no meaning for a file opened in the output mode. The setting of the current record pointer is affected only by the OPEN and READ statements.

1.2.4 I-O STATUS

If the FILE STATUS clause is specified in a file control entry, a value is placed into the specified two-character data item during the execution of an OPEN, CLOSE, READ, WRITE, or REWRITE statement to indicate to the COBOL program the status of that input-output operation.

1.2.4.1 Status Key 1

The leftmost character position of the FILE STATUS data item is known as status key 1 and is set to indicate one of the following conditions upon completion of the input-output operation.

'0' indicates Successful Completion
'1' indicates At End
'3' indicates Permanent Error
'9' indicates Implementor Defined

The meaning of the above indications are as follows:

0—Successful Completion. The input-output statement was successfully executed.

1—At End. The sequential READ statement was unsuccessfully executed as a result of an attempt to read a record when no next logical record exists in the file.

3—Permanent Error. The input-output statement was unsuccessfully executed as the result of a boundary violation for a sequential file or as the result of an input-output error, such as data check parity error, or transmission error.

9—Implementor Defined. The input-output statement was unsuccessfully executed as a result of a condition that is specified by the implementor. This value is used only to indicate a condition not indicated by other defined values of status key 1, or by specified combinations of the values of status key 1 and status key 2.

1.2.4.2 Status Key 2

The rightmost character position of the FILE STATUS data item is known as status key 2 and is used to further describe the results of the input-output operation. This character will contain a value as follows:

1. If no further information is available concerning the input-output operation, then status key 2 contains a value of '0'.

2. When status key 1 contains a value of '3' indicating a permanent error condition, status key 2 may contain a value of '4' indicating a boundary violation. This condition indicates that an attempt has been made to write beyond the externally defined boundaries of a sequential file. The implementor specifies the manner in which these boundaries are defined.

3. When status key 1 contains a value of '9' indicating an implementor-defined condition, the value of status key 2 is defined by the implementor.

1.2.4.3 Valid Combinations of Status Keys 1 and 2

The valid permissible combinations of the values of status key 1 and status key 2 are shown in Table 1. An 'X' at an intersection indicates a valid permissible combination.

1.2.5 THE AT END CONDITION

The AT END condition can occur as a result of the execution of a READ statement. For details of the causes of the condition, see paragraph 4.3, The READ Statement.

Table 1

Status Key 1	Status Key 2	
	No Further Information (0)	*Boundary Violation (4)*
Successful Completion (0)	X	
At End (1)	X	
Permanent Error (3)	X	X
Implementor Defined (9)		

2

ENVIRONMENT DIVISION IN THE SEQUEN-TIAL I-O MODULE

2.1 Input-Output Section

2.1.1 THE FILE-CONTROL PARAGRAPH

2.1.1.1 Function

The FILE-CONTROL paragraph names each file and allows specification of other file-related information.

2.1.1.2 General Format

FILE-CONTROL. {file-control-entry} . . .

2.1.2 THE FILE CONTROL ENTRY

2.1.2.1 Function

The file control entry names a file and may specify other file-related information.

2.1.2.2 General Format

SELECT file-name

        ASSIGN TO implementor-name

        [; ORGANIZATION IS SEQUENTIAL]

        [; ACCESS MODE IS SEQUENTIAL]

        [; FILE STATUS IS data-name].

2.1.2.3 Syntax Rules

(1)   The SELECT clause must be specified first in the file control entry. The clauses which follow the SELECT clause may appear in any order.

(2)   Each file described in the Data Division must be named once and only once as file-name in the FILE-CONTROL paragraph. Each file specified in the file control entry must have a file description entry in the Data Division.

(3)   If the ACCESS MODE clause is not specified, the ACCESS MODE IS SEQUENTIAL clause is implied.

(4)   Data-name must be defined in the Data Division as a two-character data item of the category alphanumeric and must not be defined in the File Section or the Communication Section.

(5)   When the ORGANIZATION IS SEQUENTIAL clause is not specified, the ORGANIZATION IS SEQUENTIAL clause is implied.

2.1.2.4 General Rules

(1)   The ASSIGN clause specifies the association of the file referenced by file-name to a storage medium.

(2)   The ORGANIZATION clause specifies the logical structure of a file. The file organization is established at the time a file is created and cannot subsequently be changed.

(3)   Records in the file are accessed in the sequence dictated by the file organization. This sequence is specified by predecessor-successor record relationships established by the execution of WRITE statements when the file is created or extended.

(4)   When the FILE STATUS clause is specified, a value will be moved by the operating system into the data item specified by data-name after the execution of every statement that references that file either explicitly or implicitly. This value indicates the status of execution of the statement. (See paragraph 1.2.4, I-O Status.)

3

DATA DIVISION IN THE SEQUENTIAL
I-O MODULE

3.1 File Section

In a COBOL program the file description entry (FD) represents the highest level of organization in the File Section. The File Section header is followed by a file description entry consisting of a level indicator (FD), a file-name and a series of independent clauses. The FD clauses specify the size of the physical records, the presence or absence of label records, and the value of implementor-defined label items. The entry itself is terminated by a period.

3.2 Record Description Structure

A record description consists of a set of data description entries which describe the characteristics of a particular record. Each data description entry consists of a level-number followed by a data-name if required, followed by a series of independent clauses as required. A record description has a hierarchical structure and therefore the clauses used with an entry may vary considerably, depending upon whether or not it is followed by subordinate entries. The structure of a record description is defined in Concept of Levels on page 79 while the elements allowed in a record description are shown in the data description skeleton on page 121.

3.3 The File Description—Complete Entry Skeleton

3.3.1 FUNCTION

The file description furnishes information concerning the physical structure and identification pertaining to a given file.

3.3.2 GENERAL FORMAT

FD file-name

$$\left[; \underline{\text{BLOCK}} \text{ CONTAINS integer } \left\{ \begin{matrix} \text{RECORDS} \\ \text{CHARACTERS} \end{matrix} \right\} \right]$$

$$; \underline{\text{LABEL}} \left\{ \begin{matrix} \underline{\text{RECORD}} \text{ IS} \\ \underline{\text{RECORDS}} \text{ ARE} \end{matrix} \right\} \left\{ \begin{matrix} \underline{\text{STANDARD}} \\ \underline{\text{OMITTED}} \end{matrix} \right\}$$

[; <u>VALUE OF</u> implementor-name IS literal].

3.3.3 SYNTAX RULES

(1) The level indicator FD identifies the beginning of a file description and must precede the file-name.

(2) The clauses which follow the name of the file are optional in many cases, and their order of appearance is immaterial.

(3) One or more record description entries must follow the file description entry.

3.4 The BLOCK CONTAINS Clause

3.4.1 FUNCTION

The BLOCK CONTAINS clause specifies the size of a physical record.

3.4.2 GENERAL FORMAT

$$\underline{\text{BLOCK}} \text{ CONTAINS integer } \left\{ \begin{matrix} \text{RECORDS} \\ \text{CHARACTERS} \end{matrix} \right\}$$

3.4.3 GENERAL RULES

(1) This clause is required except when:

(a) A physical record contains one and only one complete logical record.

(b) The hardware device assigned to the file has one and only one physical record size.

(c) The hardware device assigned to the file has more than one physical record size but the implementor has designated one as standard. In this case, the absence of this clause denotes the standard physical record size.

(2) The size of the physical record may be stated in terms of RECORDS, unless one of the following situations exists, in which case the RECORDS phrase must not be used.

(a) In mass storage files, where logical records may extend across physical records.

(b) The physical record contains padding (area not contained in a logical record).

(c) Logical records are grouped in such a manner that an inaccurate physical record size would be implied.

(3) When the word CHARACTERS is specified, the physical record size is specified in terms of the number of character positions required to store the physical record, regardless of the types of characters used to represent the items within the physical record.

(4) Integer represents the exact size of the physical record.

(5) If logical records of differing size are grouped into one physical record, the technique for determining the size of each logical record is specified by the implementor.

3.5 The LABEL RECORDS Clause

3.5.1 FUNCTION

The LABEL RECORDS clause specifies whether labels are present.

3.5.2 GENERAL FORMAT

$$\underline{\text{LABEL}} \quad \left\{ \begin{matrix} \underline{\text{RECORD}} \text{ IS} \\ \underline{\text{RECORDS}} \text{ ARE} \end{matrix} \right\} \quad \left\{ \begin{matrix} \underline{\text{STANDARD}} \\ \underline{\text{OMITTED}} \end{matrix} \right\}$$

3.5.3 SYNTAX RULES

(1) This clause is required in every file description entry.

3.5.4 GENERAL RULES

(1) OMITTED specifies that no explicit labels exist for the file or the device to which the file is assigned.

(2) STANDARD specifies that labels exist for the file or the device to which the file is assigned and the labels conform to the implementor's label specifications.

3.6 The VALUE OF Clause

3.6.1 FUNCTION

The VALUE OF clause particularizes the description of an item in the label records associated with a file.

3.6.2 GENERAL FORMAT

<u>VALUE OF</u> implementor-name IS literal

3.6.3 GENERAL RULES

(1) For an input file, the appropriate label routine checks to see if the value of implementor-name is equal to the value of literal.

For an output file, at the appropriate time the value of implementor-name is made equal to the value of literal.

(2) A figurative constant may be substituted in the format where literal is specified.

4

PROCEDURE DIVISION IN THE SEQUENTIAL I-O MODULE

4.1 The CLOSE Statement

4.1.1 Function

The CLOSE statement terminates the processing of a file.

4.1.2 GENERAL FORMAT

<u>CLOSE</u> file-name

4.1.3 GENERAL RULES

Except where otherwise stated in the general rules below, the terms 'reel' and 'unit' are synonymous and completely interchangeable in the CLOSE statement. Treatment of sequential mass storage files is logically equivalent to the treatment of a file on tape or analogous sequential media.

(1) A CLOSE statement may only be executed for a file in an open mode.

(2) For the purpose of showing the effect of various types of CLOSE statements as applied to various storage media, all files are divided into the following categories:

(a) Non-reel/unit. A file whose input or output medium is such that the concepts of rewind and reels/unit have no meaning.

(b) Sequential single-reel/unit. A sequential file that is entirely contained on one reel/unit.

(c) Sequential multi-reel/unit. A sequential file that is contained on more than one reel/unit.

(3) The results of executing the CLOSE statement for each category of file is summarized in Table 2.

The definitions of the symbols in the table are given below. Where the definition depends on whether the file is an input, output or input-output file, alternate definitions are given; otherwise, a definition applies to input, output, and input-output files.

A. *Previous Reels/Units Unaffected*

Input Files and Input-Output Files:

All reels/units in the file prior to the current reel/unit are processed according to the implementor's standard reel/unit swap procedure. If the current reel/unit is not the last in the file, the reels/units in the file following the current one are not processed.

Output Files:

All reels/units in the file prior to the current reel/unit are processed according to the implementor's standard reel/unit swap procedure.

B. *Close File*

Input Files and Input-Output Files:

If the file is positioned at its end and label records are specified for the file, the labels are processed according to the implementor's standard label convention. The behavior of the CLOSE statement when label records are specified but not present, or when label records are not specified but are present, is undefined. Closing operations specified by the implementor are

Table 2
Relationship of Categories of Files and the CLOSE Statement

CLOSE		*File Category*	
Statement *Format*	*Non-Reel/Unit*	*Sequential* *Single-* *Reel/Unit*	*Sequential* *Multi-* *Reel/Unit*
CLOSE	B	B,C	B,C,A

executed. If the file is positioned at its end and label records are not specified for the file, label processing does not take place but other closing operations specified by the implementor are executed. If the file is positioned other than at its end, the closing operations specified by the implementor are executed, but there is no ending label processing.

Output Files:

If label records are specified for the file, the labels are processed according to the implementor's standard label convention. The behavior of the CLOSE statement when label records are specified but not present, or when label records are not specified but are present, is undefined. Closing operations specified by the implementor are executed. If label records are not specified for the file, label processing does not take place but other closing operations specified by the implementor are executed.

C. *Rewind*

The current reel or analogous device is positioned at its physical beginning.

(4) The action taken if the file is in the open mode when a STOP RUN statement is executed is specified by the implementor. The action taken for a file that has been opened in a called program and not closed in that program is also specified by the implementor.

(5) If a CLOSE statement has been executed for a file, no other statement (except the SORT or MERGE statements with the USING or GIVING phrases) can be executed that references that file, either explicitly or implicitly, unless an intervening OPEN statement for that file is executed.

(6) Following the successful execution of a CLOSE statement, the record area associated with file-name is no longer available. The unsuccessful execution of such a CLOSE statement leaves the availability of the record area undefined.

4.2 The OPEN Statement

4.2.1 FUNCTION

The OPEN statement initiates the processing of files. It also performs checking and/or writing of labels and other input-output operations.

4.2.2 GENERAL FORMAT

$$\underline{\text{OPEN}} \quad \left\{ \begin{array}{l} \underline{\text{INPUT}} \text{ file-name-1} \\ \underline{\text{OUTPUT}} \text{ file-name-2} \\ \underline{\text{I-O}} \text{ file-name-3} \end{array} \right\}$$

4.2.3 SYNTAX RULES

(1)   The I-O phrase can be used only for mass storage files.

4.2.4 GENERAL RULES

(1)   The successful execution of an OPEN statement determines the availability of the file and results in the file being in an open mode.

(2)   The successful execution of an OPEN statement makes the associated record area available to the program.

(3)   Prior to the successful execution of an OPEN statement for a given file, no statement (except for a SORT statement with the USING or GIVING phrases) can be executed that references that file, either explicitly or implicitly.

(4)   An OPEN statement must be successfully executed prior to the execution of any of the permissible input-output statements. In Table 3 'X' at an intersection indicates that the specified statement, used in the sequential access mode, may be used with the sequential file organization and open mode given at the top of the column.

(5)   A file may be opened with the INPUT, OUTPUT, and I-O phrases in the same program. Following the initial execution of an

Table 3 Permissible Statements

Statement	Open Mode		
	Input	Output	Input-Output
READ	X		X
WRITE		X	
REWRITE			X

OPEN statement for a file, each subsequent OPEN statement execution for that same file must be preceded by the execution of a CLOSE statement for that file.

(6)   Execution of the OPEN statement does not obtain or release the first data record.

(7)   If label records are specified for the file, the beginning labels are processed as follows:

(a) When the INPUT phrase is specified, the execution of the OPEN statement causes the labels to be checked in accordance with the implementor's specified conventions for input label checking.

(b) When the OUTPUT phrase is specified, the execution of the OPEN statement causes the labels to be written in accordance with the implementor's specified conventions for output label writing.

The behavior of the OPEN statement when label records are specified but not present, or when label records are not specified but are present, is undefined.

(8)   The file description entry for file-name-1 or file-name-3 must be equivalent to that used when this file was created.

(9)   If the storage medium for the file permits rewinding, execution of the OPEN statement causes the file to be positioned at its beginning.

(10) For files being opened with the INPUT or I-O phrase, the OPEN statement sets the current record pointer to the first record

currently existing within the file. If no records exist in the file, the current record pointer is set such that the next executed READ statement for the file will result in an AT END condition.

(11) The I-O phrase permits the opening of a mass storage file for both input and output operations. Since this phrase implies the existence of the file, it cannot be used if the mass storage file is being initially created.

(12) When the I-O phrase is specified and the LABEL REC-ORDS clause indicates label records are present, the execution of the OPEN statement includes the following steps:

(a) The labels are checked in accordance with the implementor's specified conventions for input-output label checking.

(b) The new labels are written in accordance with the implementor's specified conventions for input-output label writing.

(13) Upon successful execution of an OPEN statement with the OUTPUT phrase specified, a file is created. At that time the associated file contains no data records.

4.3 The READ Statement

4.3.1 FUNCTION

The READ statement makes available the next logical record from a file.

4.3.2 GENERAL FORMAT

<u>READ</u> file-name RECORD; AT <u>END</u> imperative-statement

4.3.3 SYNTAX RULES

(1) The AT END phrase must be specified.

4.3.4 GENERAL RULES

(1)   The associated file must be open in the INPUT or I-O mode at the time this statement is executed. (See The OPEN Statement in paragraph 4.2.)

(2)   The record to be made available by the READ statement is determined as follows:

(a) If the current record pointer was positioned by the execution of the OPEN statement, the record pointed to by the current record pointer is made available.

(b) If the current record pointer was positioned by the execution of a previous READ statement, the current record pointer is updated to point to the next existing record in the file and then that record is made available.

(3)   The execution of the READ statement causes the value of the FILE STATUS data item, if any, associated with file-name to be updated. (See paragraph 1.2.4, I-O Status.)

(4)   Regardless of the method used to overlap access time with processing time, the concept of the READ statement is unchanged in that a record is available to the object program prior to the execution of any statement following the READ statement.

(5)   When the logical records of a file are described with more than one record description, these records automatically share the same storage area; this is equivalent to an implicit redefinition of the area. The contents of any data items which lie beyond the range of the current data record are undefined at the completion of the execution of the READ statement.

(6)   If, at the time of execution of a READ statement, the position of current record pointer for that file is undefined, the execution of that READ statement is unsuccessful.

(7)   If the end of a reel or unit is recognized during execution of a READ statement, and the logical end of the file has not been reached, the following operations are executed:

(a) The standard ending reel/unit label procedure.

(b) A reel/unit swap.

(c) The standard beginning reel/unit label procedure.

(d) The first data record of the new reel/unit is made available.

(8) If, at the time of the execution of a READ statement, no next logical record exists in the file, the AT END condition occurs, and the execution of the READ statement is considered unsuccessful. (See paragraph 1.2.4, I-O Status.)

(9) When the AT END condition is recognized the following actions are taken in the specified order:

(a) A value is placed into the FILE STATUS data item, if specified for this file, to indicate an AT END condition. (See paragraph 1.2.4, I-O Status.)

(b) Control is transferred to the AT END imperative-statement in the READ statement causing the AT END condition.

When the AT END condition occurs, execution of the input-output statement which caused the condition is unsuccessful.

(10) Following the unsuccessful execution of any READ statement, the contents of the associated record area and the position of the current record pointer are undefined.

(11) When the AT END condition has been recognized, a READ statement for that file must not be executed without first executing a successful CLOSE statement followed by the execution of a successful OPEN statement for that file.

4.4 The REWRITE Statement

4.4.1 FUNCTION

The REWRITE statement logically replaces a record existing in a mass storage file.

4.4.2 GENERAL FORMAT

REWRITE record-name

4.4.3 SYNTAX RULES

(1)   Record-name is the name of a logical record in the File Section of the Data Division and may be qualified.

4.4.4 GENERAL RULES

(1)   The file associated with record-name must be a mass storage file and must be open in the I-O mode at the time of execution of this statement. (See paragraph 4.2, The OPEN Statement.)

(2)   The last input-output statement executed for the associated file prior to the execution of the REWRITE statement must have been a successfully executed READ statement. The MSCS logically replaces the record that was accessed by the READ statement.

(3)   The number of character positions in the record referenced by record-name must be equal to the number of character positions in the record being replaced.

(4)   The logical record released by a successful execution of the REWRITE statement is no longer available in the record area.

(5)   The current record pointer is not affected by the execution of a REWRITE statement.

(6)   The execution of the REWRITE statement causes the value of the FILE STATUS data item, if any, associated with the file to be updated. (See paragraph 1.2.4, I-O Status.)

4.5 The WRITE Statement

4.5.1 FUNCTION

The WRITE statement releases a logical record for an output file. It can also be used for vertical positioning of lines within a logical page.

193

4.5.2 GENERAL FORMAT

<u>WRITE</u> record-name

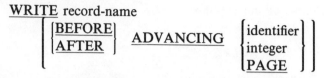

4.5.3 SYNTAX RULES

(1) The record name is the name of a logical record in the File Section of the Data Division.

(2) When identifier is used in the **ADVANCING** phrase, it must be the name of an elementary integer data item.

(3) Integer or the value of the data item referenced by identifier may be zero.

4.5.4 GENERAL RULES

(1) The associated file must be open in the OUTPUT mode at the time of the execution of this statement. (See paragraph 4.2, The OPEN Statement.)

(2) The logical record released by the execution of the WRITE statement is no longer available in the record area unless the execution of the WRITE statement was unsuccessful due to a boundary violation.

(3) The current record pointer is unaffected by the execution of a WRITE statement.

(4) The execution of the WRITE statement causes the value of the FILE STATUS data item, if any, associated with the file to be updated. (See paragraph 1.2.4, I-O Status.)

(5) The maximum record size for a file is established at the time the file is created and must not subsequently be changed.

(6) The number of character positions on a mass storage device required to store a logical record in a file may or may not be equal to the number of character positions defined by the logical description of that record in the program.

(7)   The execution of the WRITE statement releases a logical record to the operating system.

(8)   The ADVANCING phrase allows control of the vertical positioning of each line on a representation of a printed page. If the ADVANCING phrase is not used, automatic advancing will be provided by the implementor to act as if the user had specified AFTER ADVANCING 1. If the ADVANCING phrase is used, advancing is provided as follows:

(a) If identifier is specified, the representation of the printed page is advanced the number of lines equal to the current value associated with identifier.

(b) If integer is specified, the representation of the printed page is advanced the number of lines equal to the value of integer.

(c) If the BEFORE phrase is used, the line is presented before the representation of the printed page is advanced according to rules a and b above.

(d) If the AFTER phrase is used, the line is presented before the representation of the printed page is advanced according to rules a and b above.

(e) If PAGE is specified, the record is presented on the logical page before or after (depending on the phrase used) the device is repositioned to the next logical page. The repositioning to the next logical page is accomplished in accordance with an implementor-defined technique. If page has no meaning in conjunction with a specific device, then advancing will be provided by the implementor to act as if the user had specified BEFORE or AFTER (depending on the phrase used) ADVANCING 1.

(9)   When an attempt is made to write beyond the externally defined boundaries of a sequential file, an exception condition exists and the contents of the record area are unaffected. The value of the FILE STATUS data item, if any, of the associated file is set to a value indicating a boundary violation. (See paragraph 1.2.4, I-O Status.)

(10) After the recognition of an end-of-reel or an end-of-unit of an output file that is contained on more than one physical reel/unit, the WRITE statement performs the following operations:

(a) The standard ending reel/unit label procedure.

(b) A reel/unit swap.

(c) The standard beginning reel/unit label procedure.

SECTION V

Relative I-O Module

1

INTRODUCTION TO THE RELATIVE I-O MODULE

1.1 Function

The Relative I-O module in American National Standard Minimum COBOL provides a capability to access records of a mass storage file in either a random or sequential manner. Each record in a relative file is uniquely identified by an integer value greater than zero which specifies the record's logical ordinal position in the file.

1.2 Language Concepts

1.2.1 ORGANIZATION

Relative file organization is permitted only on mass storage devices. A relative file consists of records which are identified by relative record numbers. The file may be thought of as composed of a serial string of areas, each capable of holding a logical record. Each of these areas is denominated by a relative record number. Records are stored and retrieved based on this number. For example, the tenth record is the one addressed by relative record number 10 and is in the tenth record area, whether or not records have been written in the first through the ninth record areas.

1.2.2 ACCESS MODES

In the sequential access mode, the sequence in which records are accessed is the ascending order of the relative record numbers of all records which currently exist within the file.

In the random access mode, the sequence in which records are accessed is controlled by the programmer. The desired record is accessed by placing its relative record number in a relative key data item.

1.2.3 CURRENT RECORD POINTER

The current record pointer is a conceptual entity used in this document to facilitate specification of the next record to be accessed within a given file. The concept of the current record pointer has no meaning for a file opened in the output mode. The setting of the current record pointer is affected only by the OPEN and READ statements.

1.2.4 I-O STATUS

If the FILE STATUS clause is specified in a file control entry, a value is placed into the specified two-character data item during the execution of an OPEN, CLOSE, READ, WRITE, REWRITE, or DELETE statement to indicate to the COBOL program the status of that input-output operation.

1.2.4.1 Status Key 1

The leftmost character position of the FILE STATUS data item is known as status key 1 and is set to indicate one of the following conditions upon completion of the input-output operation.

'0' indicates Successful Completion
'1' indicates At End
'2' indicates Invalid Key
'3' indicates Permanent Error
'9' indicates Implementor Defined

The meaning of the above indications are as follows:

0—Successful Completion. The input-output statement was successfully executed.

1—At End. The Format 1 READ statement was unsuccessfully executed as a result of an attempt to read a record when no next logical record exists in the file.

2—Invalid Key. The input-output statement was unsuccess-fully executed as a result of one of the following:

Duplicate Key
No Record Found
Boundary Violation

3—Permanent Error. The input-output statement was un-successfully executed as the result of an input-output error, such as data check, parity error, or transmission error.

9—Implementor Defined. The input-output statement was unsuccessfully executed as a result of a condition that is specified by the implementor. This value is used only to indicate a condition not indicated by other defined values of status key 1, or by specified combinations of the values of status key 1 and status key 2.

1.2.4.2 Status Key 2

The rightmost character position of the FILE STATUS data item is known as status key 2 and is used to further describe the results of the input-output operation. This character will contain a value as follows:

1. If no further information is available concerning the in-put-output operation, then status key 2 contains a value of '0'.

2. When status key 1 contains a value of '2' indicating an INVALID KEY condition, status key 2 is used to desig-nate the cause of that condition as follows:

    a. A value of '2' in status key 2 indicates a duplicate key value. An attempt has been made to write a record that would create a duplicate key in a relative file.

    b. A value of '3' in status key 2 indicates no record found. An attempt has been made to access a rec-ord, identified by a key, and that record does not exist in the file.

c. A value of '4' in status key 2 indicates a boundary violation. An attempt has been made to write beyond the externally-defined boundaries of a relative file. The implementor specifies the manner in which these boundaries are defined.

3. When status key 1 contains a value of '9' indicating an implementor-defined condition, the value of status key 2 is defined by the implementor.

1.2.4.3 Valid Combinations of Status Keys 1 and 2

The valid permissible combinations of the values of status key 1 and status key 2 are shown in Table 1. An 'X' at an intersection indicates a valid permissible combination.

Table 1

Status Key 1	Status Key 2			
	No Further Information (0)	Duplicate Key (2)	No Record Found (3)	Boundary Violation (4)
Successful Completion (0)	X			
At End (1)	X			
Invalid Key (2)		X	X	X
Permanent Error (3)	X			
Implementor Defined (9)				

1.2.5 THE INVALID KEY CONDITION

The INVALID KEY condition can occur as a result of the execution of a READ, WRITE, REWRITE, or DELETE statement. For details of the causes of the condition, see paragraph 4.4, The READ Statement; paragraph 4.6, The WRITE Statement; paragraph 4.5, The REWRITE Statement; and paragraph 4.2, The DELETE Statement.

When the INVALID KEY condition is recognized, the MSCS takes these actions in the following order:

1. A value is placed into the FILE STATUS data item, if specified for this file, to indicate an INVALID KEY condition. (See paragraph 1.2.4, I-O Status.)

2. Control is transferred to the INVALID KEY imperative-statement within the statement causing the condition.

When the INVALID KEY condition occurs, execution of the input-output statement which recognized the condition is unsuccessful and the file is not affected.

1.2.6 THE AT END CONDITION

The AT END condition can occur as a result of the execution of a READ statement. For details of the causes of the condition, see paragraph 4.4, The READ Statement.

2

ENVIRONMENT DIVISION IN THE RELATIVE I-O MODULE

2.1 Input-Output Section

2.1.1 THE FILE-CONTROL PARAGRAPH

2.1.1.1 Function

The FILE-CONTROL paragraph names each file and allows specification of other file-related information.

2.1.1.2 General Format

FILE-CONTROL. {file-control-entry} . . .

2.1.2 THE FILE CONTROL ENTRY

2.1.2.1 Function

The file control entry names a file and may specify other file-related information.

2.1.2.2 General Format

SELECT file-name

ASSIGN TO implementor-name

; ORGANIZATION IS RELATIVE

ACCESS MODE IS

SEQUENTIAL [, RELATIVE KEY IS data-name-1]]
RANDOM, RELATIVE KEY IS data-name-1
[; FILE STATUS IS data-name-2].

2.1.2.3 Syntax Rules

(1)   The SELECT clause must be specified first in the file control entry. The clauses which follow the SELECT clause may appear in any order.

(2)   Each file described in the Data Division must be named once and only once as file-name in the FILE-CONTROL paragraph. Each file specified in the file control entry must have a file description entry in the Data Division.

(3)   If the ACCESS MODE clause is not specified, the ACCESS MODE IS SEQUENTIAL clause is implied.

(4)   Data-name-2 must be defined in the Data Division as a two-character data item of the category alphanumeric and must not be defined in the File Section or the Communication Section.

(5)   Data-name-1 must not be defined in a record description entry associated with that file-name.

(6)   The data item referenced by data-name-1 must be defined as an unsigned integer.

2.1.2.4 General Rules

(1)   The ASSIGN clause specifies the association of the file referenced by file-name to a storage medium.

(2)   The ORGANIZATION clause specifies the logical structure of a file. The file organization is established at the time a file is created and cannot subsequently be changed.

(3)   When the access mode is sequential, records in the file are accessed in the sequence dictated by the file organization. This sequence is the order of ascending relative record numbers of existing records in the file.

(4)   When the FILE STATUS clause is specified, a value will be moved by the operating system into the data item specified by data-name-2 after the execution of every statement that references that file either explicitly or implicitly. This value indicates the

status of execution of the statement. (See paragraph 1.2.4, I-O Status.)

(5)   If the access mode is random, the value of the RELATIVE KEY data item indicates the record to be accessed.

(6)   All records stored in a relative file are uniquely identified by relative record numbers. The relative record number of a given record specifies the record's logical ordinal position in the file. The first logical record has a relative record number of one (1), and subsequent logical records have relative record numbers of 2, 3, 4, ...

(7)   The data item specified by data-name-1 is used to communicate a relative record number between the user and the MSCS.

3

DATA DIVISION IN THE RELATIVE I-O MODULE

3.1 File Section

In a COBOL program the file description entry (FD) represents the highest level of organization in the File Section. The File Section header is followed by a file description entry consisting of a level indicator (FD), a file-name and a series of independent clauses. The FD clauses specify the size of the physical records, the presence or absence of label records, and the value of implementor-defined label items. The entry itself is terminated by a period.

3.2 Record Description Structure

A record description consists of a set of data description entries which describe the characteristics of a particular record. Each data description entry consists of a level-number followed by a data-name if required, followed by a series of independent clauses as required. A record description has a hierarchical structure and therefore the clauses used with an entry may vary considerably, depending upon whether or not it is followed by subordinate entries. The structure of a record description is defined in Concept of Levels on page 79 while the elements allowed in a record description are shown in the data description skeleton on page 121.

3.3 The File Description—Complete Entry Skeleton

3.3.1 FUNCTION

The file description furnishes information concerning the physical structure and identification pertaining to a given file.

3.3.2 GENERAL FORMAT

FD file-name

$$\left[;\ \underline{\text{BLOCK}}\ \text{CONTAINS integer} \begin{bmatrix} \text{RECORDS} \\ \text{CHARACTERS} \end{bmatrix} \right]$$

$$;\ \underline{\text{LABEL}} \begin{bmatrix} \underline{\text{RECORD}}\ \text{IS} \\ \underline{\text{RECORDS}}\ \text{ARE} \end{bmatrix} \begin{bmatrix} \text{STANDARD} \\ \text{OMITTED} \end{bmatrix}$$

[; VALUE OF implementor-name IS literal].

3.3.3 SYNTAX RULES

(1) The level indicator FD identifies the beginning of a file description and must precede the file-name.

(2) The clauses which follow the name of the file are optional in many cases, and their order of appearance is immaterial.

(3) One or more record description entries must follow the file description entry.

3.4 The BLOCK CONTAINS Clause

3.4.1 FUNCTION

The BLOCK CONTAINS clause specifies the size of a physical record.

3.4.2 GENERAL FORMAT

$$\underline{\text{BLOCK}}\ \text{CONTAINS integer} \begin{bmatrix} \text{RECORDS} \\ \text{CHARACTERS} \end{bmatrix}$$

3.4.3 GENERAL RULES

(1)   This clause is required except when:

(a) A physical record contains one and only one complete logical record.

(b) The hardware device assigned to the file has one and only one physical record size.

(c) The hardware device assigned to the file has more than one physical record size but the implementor has designated one as standard. In this case, the absence of this clause denotes the standard physical record size.

(2)   The size of the physical record may be stated in terms of RECORDS, unless one of the following situations exists, in which case the RECORDS phrase must not be used.

(a) Where logical records may extend across physical records.

(b) The physical record contains padding (area not contained in a logical record).

(c) Logical records are grouped in such a manner that an inaccurate physical record size would be implied.

(3)   When the word CHARACTERS is specified, the physical record size is specified in terms of the number of character positions required to store the physical record, regardless of the types of characters used to represent the items within the physical record.

(4)   Integer represents the exact size of the physical record.

(5)   If logical records of differing size are grouped into one physical record, the technique for determining the size of each logical record is specified by the implementor.

3.5 The LABEL RECORDS Clause

3.5.1 FUNCTION

The LABEL RECORDS clause specifies whether labels are present.

3.5.2 GENERAL FORMAT

$$\underline{\text{LABEL}} \quad \begin{bmatrix} \underline{\text{RECORD}} \text{ IS} \\ \underline{\text{RECORDS}} \text{ ARE} \end{bmatrix} \quad \begin{bmatrix} \underline{\text{STANDARD}} \\ \underline{\text{OMITTED}} \end{bmatrix}$$

3.5.3 SYNTAX RULES

(1) This clause is required in every file description entry.

3.5.4 GENERAL RULES

(1) OMITTED specifies that no explicit labels exist for the file or the device to which the file is assigned.

(2) STANDARD specifies that labels exist for the file or the device to which the file is assigned and the labels conform to the implementor's label specifications.

3.6 The VALUE OF Clause

3.6.1 FUNCTION

The VALUE OF clause particularizes the description of an item in the label records associated with a file.

3.6.2 GENERAL FORMAT

<u>VALUE OF</u> implementor-name IS literal

3.6.3 GENERAL RULES

(1) For an input file, the appropriate label routine checks to see if the value of implementor-name is equal to the value of literal.

For an output file, at the appropriate time the value of implementor-name is made equal to the value of literal.

(2) A figurative constant may be substituted in the format where literal is specified.

4

PROCEDURE DIVISION IN THE RELATIVE I-O MODULE

4.1 The CLOSE Statement

4.1.1 FUNCTION

The CLOSE statement terminates the processing of a file.

4.1.2 GENERAL FORMAT

<u>CLOSE</u> file-name

4.1.3 GENERAL RULES

(1) A CLOSE statement may only be executed for a file in an open mode.

(2) Relative files are classified as belong to the category of non-sequential single/multi-reel/unit. The results of executing a CLOSE on this category of file are summarized below.

Input Files and Input-Output Files (Sequential Access Mode):

If the file is positioned at its end and label records are specified for the file, the labels are processed according to the implementor's standard label convention. The behavior of the CLOSE statement when label records are specified but not present, or when label records are not specified but are present, is undefined. Closing operations specified by the implementor are executed. If the file is positioned at its end and label records are not specified for the file, label processing does not take place but other closing operations specified by the implementor are executed. If the file is positioned other than at its end, the closing operations specified by the implementor are executed, but there is no ending label processing.

Input Files and Input-Output Files (Random Access Mode);
Output Files (Random or Sequential Access Mode):

If label records are specified for the file, the labels are processed according to the implementor's standard label convention. The behavior of the CLOSE statement when label records are specified but not present, or when label records are not specified but are present, is undefined. Closing operations specified by the implementor are executed. If label records are not specified for the file, label processing does not take place but other closing operations specified by the implementor are executed.

(3)   The action taken if a file is in the open mode when a STOP RUN statement is executed is specified by the implementor. The action taken for a file that has been opened in a called program and not closed in that program is also specified by the implementor.

(4)   If a CLOSE statement has been executed for a file, no other statement can be executed that references that file, either explicitly or implicitly, unless an intervening OPEN statement for that file is executed.

(5)   Following the successful execution of a CLOSE statement, the record area associated with file-name is no longer available. The unsuccessful execution of such a CLOSE statement leaves the availability of the record area undefined.

4.2 The DELETE Statement

4.2.1 FUNCTION

The DELETE statement logically removes a record from a mass storage file.

4.2.2 GENERAL FORMAT

DELETE file-name RECORD [; INVALID KEY imperative-statement]

4.2.3 SYNTAX RULES

(1) The INVALID KEY phrase must not be specified for a DELETE statement which references a file which is in sequential access mode.

(2) The INVALID KEY phrase must be specified for a DE-LETE statement which references a file which is not in sequential access mode.

4.2.4 GENERAL RULES

(1) The associated file must be open in the I-O mode at the time of the execution of this statement. (See paragraph 4.3, The OPEN Statement.)

(2) For files in the sequential access mode, the last input-output statement executed for file-name prior to the execution of the DELETE statement must have been a successfully executed READ statement. The MSCS logically removes from the file the record that was accessed by that READ statement.

(3) For a file in random access mode, the MSCS logically removes from the file that record identified by the contents of the RELATIVE KEY data item associated with file-name. If the file does not contain the record specified by the key, and INVALID KEY condition exists. (See paragraph 1.2.5, The INVALID KEY Condition.)

(4) After the successful execution of a DELETE statement, the identified record has been logically removed from the file and can no longer be accessed.

(5) The execution of a DELETE statement does not affect the contents of the record area associated with file-name.

(6) The current record pointer is not affected by the execution of a DELETE statement.

(7) The execution of the DELETE statement causes the value of the specified FILE STATUS data item, if any, associated with file-name to be updated. (See paragraph 1.2.4, I-O Status.)

4.3 The OPEN Statement

4.3.1 FUNCTION

The OPEN statement initiates the processing of files. It also performs checking and/or writing of labels and other input-output operations.

4.3.2 GENERAL FORMAT

$$\underline{\text{OPEN}} \quad \begin{Bmatrix} \underline{\text{INPUT}} \text{ file-name-1} \\ \underline{\text{OUTPUT}} \text{ file-name-2} \\ \underline{\text{I-O}} \text{ file-name-3} \end{Bmatrix}$$

4.3.3 GENERAL RULES

(1)   The successful execution of an OPEN statement determines the availability of the file and results in the file being in an open mode.

(2)   The successful execution of the OPEN statement makes the associated record area available to the program.

(3)   Prior to the successful execution of an OPEN statement for a given file, no statement can be executed that references that file, either explicitly or implicitly.

(4)   An OPEN statement must be successfully executed prior to the execution of any of the permissible input-output statements. In Table 2 'X' at an intersection indicates that the specified statement, used in the access mode given for that row, may be used with the relative file organization and the open mode given at the top of the column.

(5)   A file may be opened with the INPUT, OUTPUT, and I-O phrases in the same program. Following the initial execution of an OPEN statement for a file, each subsequent OPEN statement execution for that same file must be preceded by the execution of a CLOSE statement for that file.

(6)   Execution of the OPEN statement does not obtain or release the first data record.

Table 2 Permissible Statements

File Access Mode	Statement	Open Mode		
		Input	Output	Input-Output
Sequential	READ	X		X
	WRITE		X	
	REWRITE			X
	DELETE			X
Random	READ	X		X
	WRITE		X	X
	REWRITE			X
	DELETE			X

(7)   If label records are specified for the file, the beginning labels are processed as follows:

(a) When the INPUT phrase is specified, the execution of the OPEN statement causes the labels to be checked in accordance with the implementor's specified conventions for input label checking.

(b) When the OUTPUT phrase is specified, the execution of the OPEN statement causes the labels to be written in accordance with the implementor's specified conventions for output label writing.

The behavior of the OPEN statement when label records are specified but not present, or when label records are not specified but are present, is undefined.

(8)   The file description entry for file-name-1 or file-name-3 must be equivalent to that used when this file was created.

(9)   For files being opened with the INPUT or I-O phrase, the OPEN statement sets the current record pointer to the first record

currently existing within the file. If no records exist in the file, the current record pointer is set such that the next executed Format 1 READ statement for the file will result in an AT END condition.

(10) The I-O phrase permits the opening of a file for both input and output operations. Since this phrase implies the existence of the file, it cannot be used if the file is being initially created.

(11) When the I-O phrase is specified and the LABEL RECORDS clause indicates label records are present, the execution of the OPEN statement includes the following steps:

(a) The labels are checked in accordance with the implementor's specified conventions for input-output label checking.

(b) The new labels are written in accordance with the implementor's specified conventions for input-output label writing.

(12) Upon successful execution of an OPEN statement with the OUTPUT phrase specified, a file is created. At that time the associated file contains no data records.

4.4 The READ Statement

4.4.1 FUNCTION

For sequential access, the READ statement makes available the next logical record from a file. For random access, the READ statement makes available a specified record from a mass storage file.

4.4.2 GENERAL FORMAT

Format 1

READ file-name RECORD; AT END imperative-statement-1

Format 2

READ file-name RECORD; INVALID KEY imperative-
statement-2

4.4.3 SYNTAX RULES

(1) Format 1 must be used for all files in sequential access mode.

(2) Format 2 is used for files in random access mode when
records are to be retrieved randomly.

(3) The INVALID KEY phrase or the AT END phrase must
be specified.

4.4.4 GENERAL RULES

(1) The associated files must be open in the INPUT or I-O mode
at the time this statement is executed. (See paragraph 4.3, The
OPEN Statement.)

(2) The record to be made available by a Format 1 READ
statement is determined as follows:

(a) The record, pointed to by the current record pointer, is
made available provided that the current record pointer was
positioned by the OPEN statement and the record is still
accessible through the path indicated by the current record
pointer; if the record is no longer accessible, which may have
been caused by the deletion of the record, the current record
pointer is updated to point to the next existing record in the
file and that record is then made available.

(b) If the current record pointer was positioned by the execution of a previous READ statement, the current record
pointer is updated to point to the next existing record in the
file and then that record is made available.

(3) The execution of the READ statement causes the value of
the FILE STATUS data item, if any, associated with file-name to
be updated. (See paragraph 1.2.4, I-O Status.)

(4) Regardless of the method used to overlap access time with processing time, the concept of the READ statement is unchanged in that a record is available to the object program prior to the execution of any statement following the READ statement.

(5) When the logical records of a file are described with more than one record description, these records automatically share the same storage area; this is equivalent to an implicit redefinition of the area. The contents of any data items which lie beyond the range of the current data record are undefined at the completion of the execution of the READ statement.

(6) If, at the time of execution of a Format 1 READ statement, the position of current record pointer for that file is undefined, the execution of that READ statement is unsuccessful.

(7) If, at the time of the execution of a Format 1 READ statement, no next logical record exists in the file, the AT END condition occurs, and the execution of the READ statement is considered unsuccessful. (See paragraph 1.2.4, I-O Status.)

(8) When the AT END condition is recognized the following actions are taken in the specified order:

(a) A value is placed into the FILE STATUS data item, if specified for this file, to indicate an AT END condition. (See paragraph 1.2.4, I-O Status.)

(b) Control is transferred to the AT END imperative-statement in the statement causing the condition.

When the AT END condition occurs, execution of the input-output statement which caused the condition is unsuccessful.

(9) Following the unsuccessful execution of any READ statement, the contents of the associated record area and the position of the current record pointer are undefined.

(10) When the AT END condition has been recognized, a Format 1 READ statement for that file must not be executed without first executing a successful CLOSE statement followed by the execution of a successful OPEN statement for that file.

(11) If the RELATIVE KEY phrase is specified, the execution of a Format 1 READ statement updates the contents of the RELATIVE KEY data item such that it contains the relative record number of the record made available.

(12) The execution of a Format 2 READ statement sets the current record pointer to, and makes available, the record whose relative record number is contained in the data item named in the RELATIVE KEY condition exists and execution of the READ statement is unsuccessful. (See paragraph 1.2.5, The INVALID KEY Condition.)

4.5 The REWRITE Statement

4.5.1 FUNCTION

The REWRITE statement logically replaces a record existing in a mass storage file.

4.5.2 GENERAL FORMAT

REWRITE record-name [; INVALID KEY imperative-statement]

4.5.3 SYNTAX RULES

(1)   Record-name is the name of a logical record in the File Section of the Data Division.

(2)   The INVALID KEY phrase must not be specified for a REWRITE statement which references a file in sequential access mode.

(3)   The INVALID KEY phrase must be specified in the REWRITE statement for files in the random access mode.

4.5.4 GENERAL RULES

(1)   The file associated with record-name must be open in the I-O mode at the time of execution of this statement. (See paragraph 4.3, The OPEN Statement.)

(2)   For files in the sequential access mode, the last input-output statement executed for the associated file prior to the execution of the REWRITE statement must have been a successfully executed READ statement. The MSCS logically replaces the record that was accessed by the READ statement.

(3)   The number of character positions in the record referenced by record-name must be equal to the number of character positions in the record being replaced.

(4)   The logical record released by a successful execution of the REWRITE statement is no longer available in the record area.

(5)   The current record pointer is not affected by the execution of a REWRITE statement.

(6)   The execution of the REWRITE statement causes the value of the FILE STATUS data item, if any, associated with the file to be updated. (See paragraph 1.2.4, I-O Status.)

(7)   For a file accessed in random access mode, the MSCS logically replaces the record specified by the contents of the RELATIVE KEY data item associated with the file. If the file does not contain the record specified by the key, the INVALID KEY condition exists. (See paragraph 1.2.5 The INVALID KEY Condition.) The updating operation does not take place and the data in the record area is unaffected.

4.6 The WRITE Statement

4.6.1 FUNCTION

The WRITE statement releases a logical record for an output or input-output file.

4.6.2 GENERAL FORMAT

WRITE record-name; INVALID KEY imperative-statement

4.6.3 SYNTAX RULES

(1)   The record-name is the name of a logical record in the File Section of the Data Division.

(2)   The INVALID KEY phrase must be specified.

4.6.4 GENERAL RULES

(1)   The associated file must be open in the OUTPUT or I-O mode at the time of the execution of this statement. (See paragraph 4.3, The OPEN Statement.)

(2)   The logical record released by the execution of the WRITE statement is no longer available in the record area unless the execution of the WRITE statement is unsuccessful due to an INVALID KEY condition.

(3)   The current record pointer is unaffected by the execution of a WRITE statement.

(4)   The execution of the WRITE statement causes the value of the FILE STATUS data item, if any, associated with the file to be updated. (See paragraph 1.2.4, I-O Status.)

(5)   The maximum record size for a file is established at the time the file is created and must not subsequently be changed.

(6)   The number of character positions on a mass storage device required to store a logical record in a file may or may not be equal to the number of character positions defined by the logical description of that record in the program.

(7)   The execution of the WRITE statement releases a logical record to the operating system.

(8)   When a file is opened in the output mode, records may be placed into the file by one of the following:

(a) If the access mode is sequential, the WRITE statement will cause a record to be released to the MSCS. The first record will have a relative record number of one (1) and subsequent records released will have relative record numbers of 2, 3, 4, ... If the RELATIVE KEY data item has been specified in the file control entry for the associated file, the relative record number of the record just released will be placed into the RELATIVE KEY data item by the MSCS during execution of the WRITE statement.

(b) If the access mode is random, prior to the execution of the WRITE statement the value of the RELATIVE KEY data item must be initialized in the program with the relative record number to be associated with the record in the record area. That record is then released to the MSCS by execution of the WRITE statement.

(9)   When a file is opened in the I-O mode and the access mode is random, records are to be inserted in the associated file. The value of the RELATIVE KEY data item must be initialized by the program with the relative record number to be associated with the record in the record area. Execution of a WRITE statement then causes the contents of the record area to be released to the MSCS.

(10) The INVALID KEY condition exists under the following circumstances:

(a) When the access mode is random and the RELATIVE KEY data item specifies a record which already exists in the file, or

(b) When an attempt is made to write beyond the externally defined boundaries of the file.

(11) When the INVALID KEY condition is recognized, the execution of the WRITE statement is unsuccessful, the contents of the record area are unaffected, and the FILE STATUS data item, if any, of the associated file is set to a value indicating the cause of the condition. Execution of the program proceeds according to the rules stated in the INVALID KEY condition in paragraph 1.2.5. (See paragraph 1.2.4, I-O Status.)

SECTION VI

Indexed I-O Module

1

INTRODUCTION TO THE INDEXED I-O MODULE

1.1 Function

The Indexed I-O module in American National Standard Minimum COBOL provides a capability to access records of a mass storage file in either a random or sequential manner. Each record in an indexed file is uniquely identified by the value of one key within that record.

1.2 Language Concepts

1.2.1 ORGANIZATION

A file whose organization is indexed is a mass storage file in which data records may be accessed by the value of a key. A record description may include one key data item, which is associated with an index. Each index provides a logical path to the data records according to the contents of a data item within each record which is the record key for that index.

The data item named in the RECORD KEY clause of the file control entry for a file is the prime record key for that file. For purposes of inserting, updating, and deleting records in a file, each record is identified solely by the value of its prime record key. This value must, therefore, be unique and must not be changed when updating the record.

1.2.2 ACCESS MODES

In the sequential access mode, the sequence in which records are accessed is the ascending order of the record key values.

In the random access mode, the sequence in which records

225

are accessed is controlled by the programmer. The desired record is accessed by placing the value of its record key in a record key data item.

1.2.3 CURRENT RECORD POINTER

The current record pointer is a conceptual entity used in this document to facilitate specification of the next record to be accessed within a given file. The concept of the current record pointer has no meaning for a file opened in the output mode. The setting of the current record pointer is affected only by the OPEN and READ statements.

1.2.4 I-O STATUS

If the FILE STATUS clause is specified in a file control entry, a value is placed into the specified two-character data item during the execution of an OPEN, CLOSE, READ, WRITE, REWRITE, or DELETE statement to indicate to the COBOL program the status of that input-output operation.

1.2.4.1 Status Key 1

The leftmost character position of the FILE STATUS data item is known as status key 1 and is set to indicate one of the following conditions upon completion of the input-output operation.

'0' indicates Successful Completion
'1' indicates At End
'2' indicates Invalid Key
'3' indicates Permanent Error
'9' indicates Implementor Defined

The meaning of the above indications are as follows:

0—Successful Completion. The input-output statement was successfully executed.

1—At End. The Format 1 READ statement was unsuccessfully executed as a result of an attempt to read a record when no next logical record exists in the file.

2—Invalid Key. The input-output statement was unsuccessfully executed as a result of one of the following:

Sequence Error
Duplicate Key
No Record Found
Boundary Violation

3—Permanent Error. The input-output statement was unsuccessful as the result of an input-output error, such as data check, parity error, or transmission error.

9—Implementor Defined. The input-output statement was unsuccessfully executed as a result of a condition that is specified by the implementor. This value is used only to indicate a condition not indicated by other defined values of status key 1, or by specified combinations of the value of status key 1 and status key 2.

1.2.4.2 Status Key 2

The rightmost character position of the FILE STATUS data item is known as status key 2 and is used to further describe the results of the input-output operation. This character will contain a value as follows:

1. If no further information is available concerning the input-output operation, then status key 2 contains a value of '0'.

2. When status key 1 contains a value of '0' indicating a successful completion, status key 2 may contain a value of '2' indicating a duplicate key. This condition indicates for a READ statement, that the key value for the current key of reference is equal to the value of that same key in the next record within the current key of reference.

3. When status key 1 contains a value of '2' indicating an INVALID KEY condition, status key 2 is used to designate the cause of that condition as follows:
   a. A value of '1' in status key 2 indicates a sequence error for a sequentially accessed indexed file. The

ascending sequence requirements of successive record key values have been violated (see The WRITE Statement in paragraph 4.6), or the prime record key value has been changed by the COBOL program between the successful execution of a READ statement and the execution of the next REWRITE statement for that file.

b. A value of '2' in status key 2 indicates a duplicate key value. An attempt has been made to write or rewrite a record that would create a duplicate key in an indexed file.

c. A value of '3' in status key 2 indicates no record found. An attempt has been made to access a record, identified by a key, and that record does not exist in the file.

d. A value of '4' in status key 2 indicates a boundary violation. An attempt has been made to write beyond the externally defined boundaries of an indexed file. The implementor specifies the manner in which these boundaries are defined.

4. When status key 1 contains a value of '9' indicating an implementor-defined condition, the value of status key 2 is defined by the implementor.

1.2.4.3 Valid Combinations of Status Keys 1 and 2

The valid permissible combinations of the value of status key 1 and status key 2 are shown in Table 1. An 'X' at an intersection indicates a valid permissible combination.

1.2.5 THE INVALID KEY CONDITION

The INVALID KEY condition can occur as a result of the execution of a READ, WRITE, REWRITE or DELETE statement. For details of the causes of the condition, see paragraph 4.4, The READ Statement; paragraph 4.6, The WRITE Statement; paragraph 4.5, The REWRITE Statement; and paragraph 4.2, The DELETE Statement.

Table 1

Status Key 1	Status Key 2				
	No Further Information (0)	Sequence Error (1)	Duplicate Key (2)	No Record Found (3)	Boundary Violation (4)
Successful Completion (0)	X		X		
At End (1)	X				
Invalid Key (2)		X	X	X	X
Permanent Error (3)	X				
Implementor Defined (9)					

When the INVALID KEY condition is recognized, the MSCS takes these actions in the following order:

1. A value is placed into the FILE STATUS data item, if specified for this file, to indicate an INVALID KEY condition. (See paragraph 1.2.4, I-O Status.)

2. Control is transferred to the INVALID KEY imperative statement in the statement causing the condition.

When the INVALID KEY condition occurs, execution of the input-output statement which recognized the condition is unsuccessful and the file is not affected.

1.2.6 THE AT END CONDITION

The AT END condition can occur as a result of the execution of a READ statement. For details of the causes of the condition, see paragraph 4.4, The READ Statement.

2

ENVIRONMENT DIVISION IN THE INDEXED I-O MODULE

2.1 Input-Output Section

2.1.1 THE FILE-CONTROL PARAGRAPH

2.1.1.1 Function

The FILE-CONTROL paragraph names each file and allows specification of other file-related information.

2.1.1.2 General Format

FILE-CONTROL. {file-control-entry} . . .

2.1.2 THE FILE CONTROL ENTRY

2.1.2.1 Function

The file control entry names a file and may specify other file-related information.

2.1.2.2 General Format

SELECT file-name

    ASSIGN TO implementor-name

    ; ORGANIZATION IS INDEXED

$$\left[; \underline{\text{ACCESS}} \text{ MODE IS } \begin{bmatrix} \text{SEQUENTIAL} \\ \text{RANDOM} \end{bmatrix} \right]$$

    ; RECORD KEY IS data-name-1

    [; FILE STATUS IS data-name-2].

2.1.2.3 Syntax Rules

(1) The SELECT clause must be specified first in the file control entry. The clauses which follow the SELECT clause may appear in any order.

(2) Each file described in the Data Division must be named once and only once as file-name in the FILE-CONTROL paragraph. Each file specified in the file control entry must have a file description entry in the Data Division.

(3) If the ACCESS MODE clause is not specified, the ACCESS MODE IS SEQUENTIAL clause is implied.

(4) Data-name-2 must be defined in the Data Division as a two-character data item of the category alphanumeric and must not be defined in the File Section or the Communication Section.

(5) The data item referenced by data-name-1 must be defined as a data item of the category alphanumeric within a record description entry associated with that file-name.

2.1.2.4 General Rules

(1) The ASSIGN clause specifies the association of the file referenced by file-name to a storage medium.

(2) The ORGANIZATION clause specifies the logical structure of a file. The file organization is established at the time a file is created and cannot subsequently be changed.

(3) When the access mode is sequential, records in the file are accessed in the sequence dictated by the file organization. For indexed files this sequence is the order of ascending record key values within a given key of reference.

(4) When the FILE STATUS clause is specified, a value will be moved by the operating system into the data item specified by data-name-2 after the execution of every statement that references that file either explicitly or implicitly. This value indicates the status of execution of the statement. (See paragraph 1.2.4, I-O Status.)

(5)   If the access mode is random, the value of the record key data item indicates the record to be accessed.

(6)   The RECORD KEY clause specifies the record key that is the prime record key for the file. The values of the prime record key must be unique among records of the file. This prime record key provides an access path to records in an indexed file.

(7)   The data description of data-name-1 as well as its relative location within a record must be the same as that used when the file was created.

3

DATA DIVISION IN THE INDEXED
I-O MODULE

3.1 File Section

In a COBOL program the file description entry (FD) represents the highest level of organization in the File Section. The File Section header is followed by a file description entry consisting of a level indicator (FD), a file-name and a series of independent clauses. The FD clauses specify the size of the physical records, the presence or absence of label records, and the value of implementor-defined label items. The entry itself is terminated by a period.

3.2 Record Description Structure

A record description consists of a set of data description entries which describe the characteristics of a particular record. Each data description entry consists of a level-number followed by a data-name if required, followed by a series of independent clauses as required. A record description has a hierarchical structure and therefore the clauses used with an entry may vary considerably, depending upon whether or not it is followed by subordinate entries. The structure of a record description is defined in Concept of Levels on page 79 while the elements allowed in a record description are shown in the data description skeleton on page 121.

3.3 The File Description—Complete Entry Skeleton

3.3.1 FUNCTION

The file description furnishes information concerning the physical structure and identification pertaining to a given file.

3.3.2 GENERAL FORMAT

FD file-name

$\left[\text{; } \underline{\text{BLOCK}} \text{ CONTAINS integer } \begin{bmatrix} \underline{\text{RECORDS}} \\ \text{CHARACTERS} \end{bmatrix} \right]$

$\text{; } \underline{\text{LABEL}} \begin{bmatrix} \underline{\text{RECORD}} \text{ IS} \\ \underline{\text{RECORDS}} \text{ ARE} \end{bmatrix} \begin{bmatrix} \underline{\text{STANDARD}} \\ \underline{\text{OMITTED}} \end{bmatrix}$

$[\text{; } \underline{\text{VALUE OF}} \text{ implementor-name IS literal}].$

3.3.3 SYNTAX RULES

(1) The level indicator FD identifies the beginning of a file description and must precede the file-name.

(2) The clauses which follow the name of the file are optional in many cases, and their order of appearance is immaterial.

(3) One or more record description entries must follow the file description entry.

3.4 The BLOCK CONTAINS Clause

3.4.1 FUNCTION

The BLOCK CONTAINS clause specifies the size of a physical record.

3.4.2 GENERAL FORMAT

$$\underline{\text{BLOCK}} \text{ CONTAINS integer } \begin{Bmatrix} \underline{\text{RECORDS}} \\ \text{CHARACTERS} \end{Bmatrix}$$

3.4.3 GENERAL RULES

(1) This clause is required except when:

(a) A physical record contains one and only one complete logical record.

(b) The hardware device assigned to the file has one and only one physical record size.

(c) The hardware device assigned to the file has more than one physical record size but the implementor has designated one as standard. In this case, the absence of this clause denotes the standard physical record size.

(2) The size of the physical record may be stated in terms of RECORDS, unless one of the following situations exists, in which case the RECORDS phrase must not be used.

(a) Where logical records may extend across physical records.

(b) The physical record contains padding (area not contained in a logical record).

(c) Logical records are grouped in such a manner that an inaccurate physical record size would be implied.

(3) When the word CHARACTERS is specified, the physical record size is specified in terms of the number of character positions required to store the physical record, regardless of the types of characters used to represent the items within the physical record.

(4) Integer represents the exact size of the physical record.

(5) If logical records of differing size are grouped into one physical record, the technique for determining the size of each logical record is specified by the implementor.

3.5 The LABEL RECORDS Clause

3.5.1 FUNCTION

The LABEL RECORDS clause specifies whether labels are present.

3.5.2 GENERAL FORMAT

$$\text{\underline{LABEL}} \quad \begin{Bmatrix} \text{\underline{RECORD}} \text{ IS} \\ \text{\underline{RECORDS}} \text{ ARE} \end{Bmatrix} \quad \begin{Bmatrix} \text{\underline{STANDARD}} \\ \text{\underline{OMITTED}} \end{Bmatrix}$$

3.5.3 SYNTAX RULES

(1) This clause is required in every file description entry.

3.5.4 GENERAL RULES

(1) OMITTED specifies that no explicit labels exist for the file or the device to which the file is assigned.

(2) STANDARD specifies that labels exist for the file or the device to which the file is assigned and the labels conform to the implementor's label specifications.

3.6 The VALUE OF Clause

3.6.1 FUNCTION

The VALUE OF clause particularizes the description of an item in the label records associated with a file.

3.6.2 GENERAL FORMAT

<u>VALUE OF</u> implementor-name IS literal

3.6.3 GENERAL RULES

(1)   For an input file, the appropriate label routine checks to see if the value of implementor-name is equal to the value of literal.

   For an output file, at the appropriate time the value of implementor-name is made equal to the value of literal.

(2)   A figurative constant may be substituted in the format where literal is specified.

4

PROCEDURE DIVISION IN THE INDEXED I-O MODULE

4.1 The CLOSE Statement

4.1.1 FUNCTION

The CLOSE statement terminates the processing of files.

4.1.2 GENERAL FORMAT

<u>CLOSE</u> file-name

4.1.3 GENERAL RULES

(1) A CLOSE statement may only be executed for a file in an open mode.

(2) Indexed files are classified as belonging to the category of non-sequential single/multi-reel/unit. The results of executing a CLOSE on this category of file are summarized below.

Input Files and Input-Output Files (Sequential Access Mode):
If the file is positioned at its end and label records are specified for the file, the labels are processed according to the implementor's standard label convention. The behavior of the CLOSE statement when label records are specified but not present, or when label records are not specified but are present, is undefined. Closing operations specified by the implementor are executed. If the file is positioned at its end and label records are not specified for the file, label processing does not take place but other closing operations specified by the implementor are executed. If the file is positioned other than at its end, the closing operations specified by the implementor are executed, but there is no ending label processing.

Input Files and Input-Output Files (Random Access Mode):
Output Files (Random or Sequential Access Mode):

If label records are specified for the file, the labels are processed according to the implementor's standard label convention. The behavior of the CLOSE Statement when label records are specified but not present, or when label records are not specified but are present, is undefined. Closing operations specified by the implementor are executed. If label records are not specified for the file, label processing does not take place but other closing operations specified by the implementor are executed.

(3) The action taken if the file is in the open mode when a STOP RUN statement is executed is specified by the implementor. The action taken for a file that has been opened in a called program and not closed in that program is also specified by the implementor.

(4) If a CLOSE statement has been executed for a file, no other statement can be executed that references that file, either explicitly or implicitly, unless an intervening OPEN statement for that file is executed.

(5) Following the successful execution of a CLOSE statement, the record area associated with file-name is no longer available. The unsuccessful execution of such a CLOSE statement leaves the availability of the record area undefined.

4.2 The DELETE Statement

4.2.1 FUNCTION

The DELETE statement logically removes a record from a mass storage file.

4.2.2 GENERAL FORMAT

DELETE file-name RECORD [; INVALID KEY impera-
tive-statement]

4.2.3 SYNTAX RULES

(1) The INVALID KEY phrase must not be specified for a DELETE statement which references a file which is in sequential access mode.

(2) The INVALID KEY phrase must be specified for a DELETE statement which references a file which is not in sequential access mode.

4.2.4 GENERAL RULES

(1) The associated file must be open in the I-O mode at the time of the execution of this statement. (See paragraph 4.3, The OPEN Statement.)

(2) For files in the sequential access mode, the last input-output statement executed for file-name prior to the execution of the DELETE statement must have been a successfully executed READ statement. The MSCS logically removes from the file the record that was accessed by that READ statement.

(3) For a file in random access mode, the MSCS logically removes from the file the record identified by the contents of the prime record key data item associated with file-name. If the file does not contain the record specified by the key, an INVALID KEY condition exists. (See paragraph 1.2.5, The INVALID KEY Condition.)

(4) After the successful execution of a DELETE statement, the identified record has been logically removed from the file and can no longer be accessed.

(5) The execution of a DELETE statement does not affect the contents of the record area associated with file-name.

(6) The current record pointer is not affected by the execution of a DELETE statement.

(7) The execution of the DELETE statement causes the value of the specified FILE STATUS data item, if any, associated with file-name to be updated. (See paragraph 1.2.4, I-O Status.)

4.3 The OPEN Statement

4.3.1 FUNCTION

The OPEN statement initiates the processing of files. It also performs checking and/or writing of labels and other input-output operations.

4.3.2 GENERAL FORMAT

$$\underline{OPEN} \quad \left\{ \begin{array}{l} \underline{INPUT} \text{ file-name-1} \\ \underline{OUTPUT} \text{ file-name-2} \\ \underline{I\text{-}O} \text{ file-name-3} \end{array} \right\}$$

4.3.3 GENERAL RULES

(1)   The successful execution of an OPEN statement determines the availability of the file and results in the file being in an open mode.

(2)   The successful execution of the OPEN statement makes the associated record area available to the program.

(3)   Prior to the successful execution of an OPEN statement for a given file, no statement can be executed that references that file, either explicitly or implicitly.

(4)   An OPEN statement must be successfully executed prior to the execution of any of the permissible input-output statements. In Table 2 'X' at an intersection indicates that the specified statement, used in the access mode given for that row, may be used with the indexed file organization and the open mode given at the top of the column.

(5)   A file may be opened with the INPUT, OUTPUT, and I-O phrases in the same program. Following the initial execution of an OPEN statement for a file, each subsequent OPEN statement execution for that same file must be preceded by the execution of a CLOSE statement for that file.

(6)   Execution of the OPEN statement does not obtain or release the first data record.

Table 2 Permissible Statements

File Access Mode	Statement	Open Mode		
		Input	Output	Input-Output
Sequential	READ	X		X
	WRITE		X	
	REWRITE			X
	DELETE			X
Random	READ	X		X
	WRITE		X	
	REWRITE			X
	DELETE			X

(7) If label records are specified for the file, the beginning labels are processed as follows:

(a) When the INPUT phrase is specified, the execution of the OPEN statement causes the labels to be checked in accordance with the implementor's specified conventions for input label checking.

(b) When the OUTPUT phrase is specified, the execution of the OPEN statement causes the labels to be written in accordance with the implementor's specified conventions for output label writing.

The behavior of the OPEN statement when label records are specified but not present, or when label records are not specified but are present, is undefined.

(8) The file description entry for file-name-1 or file-name-3 must be equivalent to that used when this file was created.

(9) For files being opened with the INPUT or I-O phrase, the OPEN statement sets the current record pointer to the first record

currently existing within the file. For indexed files, the prime record key is established as the key of reference and is used to determine the first record to be accessed. If no records exist in the file, the current record pointer is set such that the next executed Format 1 READ statement for the file will result in an AT END condition.

(10) The I-O phrase permits the opening of a file for both input and output operations. Since this phrase implies the existence of the file, it cannot be used if the file is being initially created.

(11) When the I-O phrase is specified and the LABEL REC-ORDS clause indicates label records are present, the execution of the OPEN statement includes the following steps:

(a) The labels are checked in accordance with the implementor's specified conventions for input-output label checking.

(b) The new labels are written in accordance with the implementor's specified conventions for input-output label writing.

(12) Upon successful execution of an OPEN statement with the OUTPUT phrase specified, a file is created. At that time the associated file contains no data records.

4.4 The READ Statement

4.4.1 FUNCTION

For sequential access, the READ statement makes available the next logical record from a file. For random access, the READ statement makes available a specified record from a mass storage file.

4.4.2 GENERAL FORMAT

Format 1

READ file-name RECORD; AT END imperative-state-ment-1

Format 2

READ file-name RECORD; INVALID KEY imperative-statement-2

4.4.3 SYNTAX RULES

(1) Format 1 must be used for all files in sequential access mode.

(2) Format 2 is used for files in random access mode when records are to be retrieved randomly.

(3) The INVALID KEY phrase or the AT END phrase must be specified.

4.4.4 GENERAL RULES

(1) The associated file must be open in the INPUT or I-O mode at the time this statement is executed. (See paragraph 4.3, The OPEN Statement.)

(2) The record to be made available for a Format 1 READ statement is determined as follows:

(a) The record, pointed to by the current record pointer, is made available provided that the current record pointer was positioned by the OPEN statement and the record is still accessible through the path indicated by the current record pointer; if the record is no longer accessible, which may have been caused by the deletion of the record, the current record pointer is updated to point to the next existing record within the established key of reference and that record is then made available.

(b) If the current record pointer was positioned by the execution of a previous READ statement, the current record pointer is updated to point to the next existing record in the file with the established key of reference and then that record is made available.

(3) The execution of the READ statement causes the value of the FILE STATUS data item, if any, associated with file-name to be updated. (See paragraph 1.2.4, I-O Status.)

(4)   Regardless of the method used to overlap access time with processing time, the concept of the READ statement is unchanged in that a record is available to the object program prior to the execution of any statement following the READ statement.

(5)   When the logical records of a file are described with more than one record description, these records automatically share the same storage area; this is equivalent to an implicit redefinition of the area. The contents of any data items which lie beyond the range of the current data record are undefined at the completion of the execution of the READ statement.

(6)   If, at the time of execution of a Format 1 READ statement, the position of current record pointer for that file is undefined, the execution of that READ statement is unsuccessful.

(7)   If, at the time of the execution of a Format 1 READ statement, no next logical record exists in the file, the AT END condition occurs, and the execution of the READ statement is considered unsuccessful. (See paragraph 1.2.4, I-O Status.)

(8)   When the AT END condition is recognized the following actions are taken in the specified order:

(a) A value is placed into the FILE STATUS data item, if specified for this file, to indicate an AT END condition. (See paragraph 1.2.4, I-O Status.)

(b) Control is transferred to the AT END imperative statement in the statement causing the AT END condition.

When the AT END condition occurs, execution of the input-output statement which caused the condition is unsuccessful.

(9)   Following the unsuccessful execution of any READ statement, the contents of the associated record area and the position of the current record pointer are undefined. For indexed files the key of reference is also undefined.

(10) When the AT END condition has been recognized, a Format 1 READ statement for that file must not be executed without first executing a successful CLOSE statement followed by the execution of a successful OPEN statement for that file.

(11) In a Format 2 READ statement, the prime record key is established as the key of reference for this retrieval.

(12) Execution of a Format 2 statement causes the value of the key of reference to be compared with the value contained in the corresponding data item of the stored records in the file, until the first record having an equal value is found. The current record pointer is positioned to this record which is then made available. If no record can be so identified, the INVALID KEY condition exists and execution of the READ statement is unsuccessful. (See paragraph 1.2.5, The INVALID KEY Condition.)

4.5 The REWRITE Statement

4.5.1 FUNCTION

The REWRITE statement logically replaces a record existing in a mass storage file.

4.5.2 GENERAL FORMAT

REWRITE record-name; INVALID KEY imperative-statement

4.5.3 SYNTAX RULES

(1) Record-name is the name of a logical record in the File Section of the Data Division.

(2) The INVALID KEY phrase must be specified in the RE-WRITE statement.

4.5.4 GENERAL RULES

(1) The file associated with record-name must be open in the I-O mode at the time of execution of this statement. (See paragraph 4.3, The OPEN Statement.)

(2)   For files in the sequential access mode, the last input-output statement executed for the associated file prior to the execution of the REWRITE statement must have been a successfully executed READ statement. The MSCS logically replaces the record that was accessed by the READ statement.

(3)   The number of character positions in the record referenced by record-name must be equal to the number of character positions in the record being replaced.

(4)   The logical record released by a successful execution of the REWRITE statement is no longer available in the record area.

(5)   The current record pointer is not affected by the execution of a REWRITE statement.

(6)   The execution of the REWRITE statement causes the value of the FILE STATUS data item, if any, associated with the file to be updated. (See paragraph 1.2.4, I-O Status.)

(7)   For a file in the sequential access mode, the record to be replaced is specified by the value contained in the prime record key. When the REWRITE statement is executed the value contained in the prime record key data item of the record to be replaced must be equal to the value of the prime record key of the last record read from this file.

(8)   For a file in the random access mode, the record to be replaced is specified by the prime record key data item.

(9)   The INVALID KEY condition exists when:

(a) The access mode is sequential and the value contained in the prime record key data item of the record to be replaced is not equal to the value of the prime record key of the last record read from this file, or

(b) The value contained in the prime record key data item does not equal that of any record stored in the file.

The updating operation does not take place and the data in the record area is unaffected. (See paragraph 1.2.5, The INVALID KEY Condition.)

4.6 The WRITE Statement

4.6.1 FUNCTION

The WRITE statement releases a logical record for an output or input-output file.

4.6.2 GENERAL FORMAT

<u>WRITE</u> record-name; <u>INVALID</u> KEY imperative-statement

4.6.3 SYNTAX RULES

(1) The record-name is the name of a logical record in the File Section of the Data Division.

(2) The INVALID KEY phrase may be specified.

4.6.4 GENERAL RULES

(1) The associated file must be open in the OUTPUT or I-O mode at the time of the execution of this statement. (See paragraph 4.3, The OPEN Statement.)

(2) The logical record released by the execution of the WRITE statement is no longer available in the record area unless the execution of the WRITE statement is unsuccessful due to an INVALID KEY condition.

(3) The current record pointer is unaffected by the execution of a WRITE statement.

(4) The execution of the WRITE statement causes the value of the FILE STATUS data item, if any, associated with the file to be updated. (See paragraph 1.2.4, I-O Status.)

(5) The maximum record size for a file is established at the time the file is created and must not subsequently be changed.

(6)   The number of character positions on a mass storage device required to store a logical record in a file may or may not be equal to the number of character positions defined by the logical description of that record in the program.

(7)   The execution of the WRITE statement releases a logical record to the operating system.

(8)   Execution of the WRITE statement causes the contents of the record area to be released. The MSCS utilizes the content of the record keys in such a way that subsequent access of the record key may be made based upon any of these specified record keys.

(9)   The value of the prime record key must be unique within the records in the file.

(10) The data item specified as the prime record key must be set by the program to the desired value prior to the execution of the WRITE statement.

(11) If sequential access mode is specified for the file, records must be released to the MSCS in ascending order of prime record key values.

(12) If random access mode is specified, records may be released to the MSCS in any program-specified order.

(13) The INVALID KEY condition exists under the following circumstances:

(a) When sequential access mode is specified for a file opened in the output mode, and the value of the prime record key is not greater than the value of the prime record key of the previous record, or

(b) When the file is opened in the output or I-O mode, and the value of the prime record key is equal to the value of a prime record key of a record already existing in the file, or

(c) When an attempt is made to write beyond the externally defined boundaries of the file.

(14) When the INVALID KEY condition is recognized the execution of the WRITE statement is unsuccessful, the contents of the record area are unaffected and the FILE STATUS data item, if any, associated with file-name of the associated file is set to a value indicating the cause of the condition. Execution of the program proceeds according to the rules stated in paragraph 1.2.5, The INVALID KEY Condition. (See paragraph 1.2.4, I-O Status.)

SECTION VII

Sort-Merge Module

1

INTRODUCTION TO THE SORT-MERGE MODULE

1.1 Function

The Sort-Merge module provides the capability to order one or more files of records according to a set of user-specified keys contained within each record. Optionally, a user may apply some special processing to each of the individual records by input or output procedures. This special processing may be applied before and/or after the records are ordered by the SORT.

1.2 Relationship with Sequential I-O Module

The files specified in the USING and GIVING phrases of the SORT statements must be described implicitly or explicitly in the FILE-CONTROL paragraph as having sequential organization. No input-output statements may be executed for the file named in the sort-merge file description.

2

ENVIRONMENT DIVISION IN THE SORT-MERGE MODULE

2.1 Input-Output Section

2.1.1 THE FILE-CONTROL PARAGRAPH

2.1.1.1 Function

The FILE-CONTROL paragraph names each file and allows specification of other file-related information.

2.1.1.2 General Format

FILE-CONTROL. {file-control-entry} . . .

2.1.2 THE FILE CONTROL ENTRY

2.1.2.1 Function

The file control entry names a sort file and specifies the association of the file to a storage medium.

2.1.2.2 General Format

SELECT file-name ASSIGN TO implementor-name.

2.1.2.3 Syntax Rules

(1) Each sort file described in the Data Division must be named once and only once as file-name in the FILE-CONTROL paragraph. Each sort file specified in the file control entry must have a sort-merge file description entry in the Data Division.

(2) Since file-name represents a sort file, only the ASSIGN clause is permitted to follow file-name in the FILE-CONTROL paragraph.

2.1.2.4 General Rules

(1) The ASSIGN clause specifies the association of the sort file referenced by file-name to a storage medium.

3

DATA DIVISION IN THE SORT-MERGE MODULE

3.1 File Section

An SD file description identifies the file to be sorted. There are no label procedures which the user can control, and the rules for blocking and internal storage are peculiar to the SORT statement.

3.2 The Sort-Merge File Description—Complete Entry Skeleton

3.2.1 FUNCTION

The sort-merge file description identifies the file-name of the file to be sorted.

3.2.2 GENERAL FORMAT

SD file-name.

3.2.3 SYNTAX RULES

(1)   The level indicator SD identifies the beginning of the sort-merge file description and must precede the file-name.

(2)   One or more record description entries must follow the sort-merge file description entry, however, no input-output statements may be executed for this file.

4

PROCEDURE DIVISION IN THE SORT-MERGE MODULE

4.1 The RELEASE Statement

4.1.1 FUNCTION

The RELEASE statement transfers records to the initial phase of a SORT operation.

4.1.2 GENERAL FORMAT

RELEASE record-name

4.1.3 SYNTAX RULES

(1)   A RELEASE statement may only be used within the range of an input procedure associated with a SORT statement for a file whose sort-merge file description entry contains record-name. (See paragraph 4.3, The SORT Statement.)

(2)   Record-name must be the name of a logical record in the associated sort-merge file description entry.

4.1.4 GENERAL RULES

(1)   The execution of a RELEASE statement causes the record named by record-name to be released to the initial phase of a sort operation.

(2)   After the execution of the RELEASE statement, the logical record is no longer available in the record area. When control passes from the input procedure, the file consists of all those records which were placed in it by the execution of RELEASE statements.

4.2 The RETURN Statement

4.2.1 FUNCTION

The RETURN statement obtains sorted records from the final phase of a SORT operation.

4.2.2 GENERAL FORMAT

RETURN file-name RECORD; AT END imperative-statement

4.2.3 SYNTAX RULES

(1) File-name must be described by a sort-merge file description entry in the Data Division.

(2) A RETURN statement may only be used within the range of an output procedure associated with a SORT statement for file-name.

(3) Imperative-statement represents one or more imperative statements.

4.2.4 GENERAL RULES

(1) When the logical records of a file are described with more than one record description, these records automatically share the same storage area; this is equivalent to an implicit redefinition of the area. The contents of any data items which lie beyond the range of the current data record area undefined at the completion of the execution of the RETURN statement.

(2) The execution of the RETURN statement causes the next record, in the order specified by the keys listed in the SORT statement, to be made available for processing in the record areas associated with the sort file.

(3) If no next logical record exists for the file at the time of the execution of a RETURN statement, the AT END condition occurs. The contents of the record areas associated with the file when

the AT END condition occurs are undefined. After the execution of the imperative-statement in the AT END phrase, no RETURN statement may be executed as part of the current output procedure.

4.3 The SORT Statement

4.3.1 FUNCTION

The SORT statement creates a sort file by executing input procedures or by transferring records from another file, sorts the records in the sort file on a set of specified keys, and in the final phase of the sort operation, makes available each record from the sort file, in sorted order, to some output procedures or to an output file.

4.3.2 GENERAL FORMAT

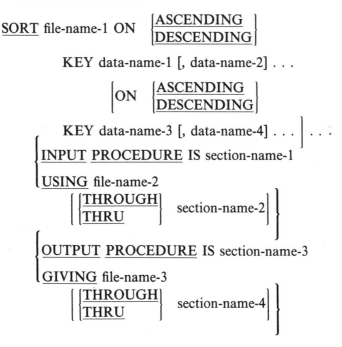

$$\underline{\text{SORT}}\ \text{file-name-1}\ \underline{\text{ON}}\ \left\{\begin{matrix}\underline{\text{ASCENDING}} \\ \underline{\text{DESCENDING}}\end{matrix}\right\}$$

$$\underline{\text{KEY}}\ \text{data-name-1}\ [,\ \text{data-name-2}]\ \ldots$$

$$\left[\underline{\text{ON}}\ \left\{\begin{matrix}\underline{\text{ASCENDING}} \\ \underline{\text{DESCENDING}}\end{matrix}\right\}\right.$$

$$\left.\underline{\text{KEY}}\ \text{data-name-3}\ [,\ \text{data-name-4}]\ \ldots\right]\ \ldots$$

$$\left\{\begin{matrix}\underline{\text{INPUT PROCEDURE}}\ \text{IS}\ \text{section-name-1} \\[6pt] \underline{\text{USING}}\ \text{file-name-2}\end{matrix}\right.$$

$$\left[\left\{\begin{matrix}\underline{\text{THROUGH}} \\ \underline{\text{THRU}}\end{matrix}\right\}\ \text{section-name-2}\right]$$

$$\left\{\begin{matrix}\underline{\text{OUTPUT PROCEDURE}}\ \text{IS}\ \text{section-name-3} \\[6pt] \underline{\text{GIVING}}\ \text{file-name-3}\end{matrix}\right.$$

$$\left[\left\{\begin{matrix}\underline{\text{THROUGH}} \\ \underline{\text{THRU}}\end{matrix}\right\}\ \text{section-name-4}\right]$$

259

4.3.3 SYNTAX RULES

(1) File-name-1 must be described in a sort-merge file description entry in the Data Division.

(2) Section-name-1 represents the name of an input procedure. Section-name-3 represents the name of an output procedure.

(3) File-name-2 and file-name-3 must be described in a file description entry, not in a sort-merge file description entry, in the Data Division. The actual size of the logical record(s) described for file-name-2 and file-name-3 must be equal to the actual size of the logical record(s) described for file-name-1. If the data descriptions of the elementary items that make up these records are not identical, it is the programmer's responsibility to describe the corresponding records in such a manner so as to cause equal amounts of character positions to be allocated for the corresponding records.

(3) Data-name-1, data-name-2, data-name-3, and data-name-4 are KEY data-names and are subject to the following rules:

(a) The data items identified by KEY data-names must be described in records associated with file-name-1.

(b) If file-name-1 has more than one record description, then the data items identified by KEY data-names need be described in only one of the record descriptions.

(c) None of the data items identified by KEY data-names can be described by an entry which either contains an OCCURS clause or is subordinate to an entry which contains an OCCURS clause.

(5) The words THRU and THROUGH are equivalent.

(6) SORT statements may appear anywhere except in an input or output procedure associated with a SORT statement.

4.3.4 GENERAL RULES

(1) The Procedure Division may contain more than one SORT statement appearing anywhere except in the input and output procedures associated with a SORT statement.

(2)   The data-names following the word KEY are listed from left to right in the SORT statement in order of decreasing significance without regard to how they are divided into KEY phrases. In the format, data-name-1 is the major key, data-name-2 is the next most significant key, etc.

(a) When the ASCENDING phrase is specified, the sorted sequence will be from the lowest value of the contents of the data items identified by the KEY data-names to the highest value, according to the rules for comparison of operands in a relation condition.

(b) When the DESCENDING phrase is specified, the sorted sequence will be from the highest value of the contents of the data items identified by the KEY data-names to the lowest value, according to the rules for comparison of operands in a relation condition.

(3)   The collating sequence that applies to the comparison of the nonnumeric key data items specified is determined by the collating sequence established as the program collating sequence.

(4)   The input procedure must consist of one or more sections that appear contiguously in a source program and do not form a part of any output procedure. In order to transfer records to the file referenced by file-name-1, the input procedure must include the execution of at least one RELEASE statement. Control must not be passed to the input procedure except when a related SORT statement is being executed. The input procedure can include any procedures needed to select, create, or modify records. The restrictions on the procedural statements within the input procedure are as follows:

(a) The input procedure must not contain any SORT statements.

(b) The input procedure must not contain any explicit transfers of control to points outside the input procedure; GO TO and PERFORM statements in the input procedure are not permitted to refer to procedure-names outside the input procedure.

(c) The remainder of the Procedure Division must not contain any transfers of control to points inside the input procedure; GO TO and PERFORM statements in the remainder of the Procedure Division must not refer to procedure-names within the input procedure.

(5)   If an input procedure is specified, control is passed to the input procedure before file-name-1 is sequenced by the SORT statement. The compiler inserts a return mechanism at the end of the last section in the input procedure and when control passes the last statement in the input procedure, the records that have been released to file-name-1 are sorted.

(6)   The output procedure must consist of one or more sections that appear contiguously in a source program and do not form part of any input procedure. In order to make sorted records available for processing, the output procedure must include the execution of at least one RETURN statement. Control must not be passed to the output procedure except when a related SORT statement is being executed. The output procedure may consist of any procedures needed to select, modify or copy the records that are being returned, one at a time in sorted order, from the sort file. The restrictions on the procedural statements within the output procedure are as follows:

(a) The output procedure must not contain any SORT statements.

(b) The output procedure must not contain any explicit transfers of control to points outside the output procedure; GO TO and PERFORM statements in the output procedure are not permitted to refer to procedure-names outside the output procedure.

(c) The remainder of the Procedure Division must not contain any transfers of control to points inside the output procedure; GO TO and PERFORM statements in the remainder of the Procedure Division are not permitted to refer to procedure-names within the output procedure.

(7)   If an output procedure is specified, control passes to it after file-name-1 has been sequenced by the SORT statement. The com-

piler inserts a return mechanism at the end of the last section in the output procedure and when control passes the last statement in the output procedure, the return mechanism provides for termination of the sort and then passes control to the next executable statement after the SORT statement. Before entering the output procedure, the sort procedure reaches a point at which it can select the next record in sorted order when requested. The RETURN statements in the output procedure are the requests for the next record.

(8) Segmentation as defined in Section VIII can be applied to programs containing the SORT statement. However, the following restrictions apply:

(a) If a SORT statement appears in a section that is not in an independent segment, then any input procedures or output procedures referenced by that SORT statement must appear:

1. Totally within non-independent segments, or
2. Wholly contained in a single independent segment.

(b) If a SORT statement appears in an independent segment, then any input procedures or output procedures referenced by that SORT statement must be contained:

1. Totally within non-independent segments, or
2. Wholly within the same independent segment as that SORT statement.

(9) If the USING phrase is specified, all the records in file-name-2 are transferred automatically to file-name-1. At the time of execution of the SORT statement, file-name-2 must not be open. The SORT statement automatically initiates the processing of, makes available the logical records for, and terminates the processing of file-name-2. The terminating function for all files is performed as if a CLOSE statement had been executed for each file. The SORT statement also automatically performs the implicit functions of moving the records from the file area of file-name-2 to the file area for file-name-1 and the release of records to the initial phrase of the sort operation.

(10) If the GIVING phrase is specified, all the sorted records in file-name-1 are automatically written on file-name-3 as the implied output procedure for this SORT statement. At the time of execution of the SORT statement file-name-3 must not be open. The SORT statement automatically initiates the processing of, releases the logical records to, and terminates the processing of file-name-3. The terminating function is performed as if a CLOSE statement has been executed for the file. The SORT statement also automatically performs the implicit functions of the return of the sorted records from the final phase of the sort operation and the moving of the records from the file area for file-name-1 to the file area for file-name-3.

Segmentation Module

1

INTRODUCTION TO THE SEGMENTATION MODULE

1.1 Function

The Segmentation module provides a capability to specify object program overlay requirements.

2

GENERAL DESCRIPTION OF SEGMENTATION

COBOL segmentation is a facility that provides a means by which the user may communicate with the compiler to specify object program overlay requirements.

2.1 Scope

COBOL segmentation deals only with segmentation of procedures. As such, only the Procedure Division and the Environment Division are considered in determining segmentation requirements for an object program.

2.2 Organization

2.2.1 PROGRAM SEGMENTS

Although it is not mandatory, the Procedure Division for a source program is usually written as a consecutive group of sections, each of which is composed of a series of closely related operations that are designed to collectively perform a particular function. However, when segmentation is used, the entire Procedure Division must be in sections. In addition, each section must be classified as belonging either to the fixed portion or to one of the independent segments of the object program. Segmentation in no way affects the need for qualification of procedure-names to insure uniqueness.

2.2.2 FIXED PORTION

The fixed portion is defined as that part of the object program which is logically treated as if it were always in memory. This portion of the program is composed of fixed permanent segments. A fixed permanent segment is a segment in the fixed portion which cannot be overlaid by any other part of the program.

2.2.3 INDEPENDENT SEGMENTS

An independent segment is defined as part of the object program which can overlay, and can be overlaid by, another independent segment. An independent segment is in its initial state whenever control is transferred (either implicitly or explicitly) to that segment for the first time during the execution of a program. On subsequent transfers of control to the segment, an independent segment is also in its initial state when:

1. Control is transferred to that segment as a result of the implicit transfer of control between consecutive statements from a segment with a different segment-number.

2. Control is transferred to that segment as the result of the implicit transfer of control between a SORT statement, in a segment with a different segment-number, and an associated input or output procedure in that independent segment.

3. Control is transferred explicitly to that segment from a segment with a different segment-number (with the exception noted in paragraph 2 below).

On subsequent transfer of control to the segment, an independent segment is in its last-used state when:

(1) Control is transferred implicitly to that segment from a segment with a different segment-number (except as noted in paragraphs 1 and 2 above).

(2) Control is transferred explicitly to that segment as the result of the execution of an EXIT PROGRAM statement.

See paragraph 5.3.4.2, Explicit and Implicit Transfers of Control in Section I.

2.3 Segmentation Classification

Sections which are to be segmented are classified, using a system of segment-numbers (see paragraph 3.1) and the following criteria:

(1) Logic Requirements—Section which must be available for reference at all times, or which are referred to very frequently, are normally classified as belonging to one of the permanent segment; sections which are used less frequently are normally classified as belonging to one of the independent segments, depending on logic requirements.

(2) Frequency of Use—Generally, the more frequently a section is referred to, the lower its segment-number, the less frequently it is referred to, the higher its segment-number.

(3) Relationship to Other Sections—Sections which frequently communicate with one another should be given the same segment-numbers.

2.4 Segmentation Control

The logical sequence of the program is the same as the physical sequence except for specific transfers of control. If any reordering of the object program is required to handle the flow from segment to segment, according to the rules in paragraph 3.1, the implementor must provide control transfers to maintain the logical flow specified in the source program. The implementor must also provide all controls necessary for a segment to operate whenever the segment is used. Control may be transferred within a source program to any paragraph in a section; that is, it is not mandatory to transfer control to the beginning of a section.

3

STRUCTURE OF PROGRAM SEGMENTS

3.1 Segment-Numbers

Section classification is accomplished by means of a system of segment-numbers. The segment-number is included in the section header.

3.1.1 GENERAL FORMAT

section-name <u>SECTION</u> [segment-number].

3.1.2 SYNTAX RULES

(1) The segment-number must be an integer ranging in value from 0 through 99.

(2) If the segment-number is omitted from the section header, the segment-number is assumed to be 0.

3.1.3 GENERAL RULES

(1) All sections which have the same segment-number constitute a program segment. All sections which have the same segment-number must be together in the source program.

(2) Segments with segment-number 0 through 49 belong to the fixed portion of the object program. All sections with segment-number 0 through 49 must be together in the source program.

(3) Segments with segment-number 50 through 99 are independent segments.

4

RESTRICTIONS ON PROGRAM FLOW

When segmentation is used, the following restrictions are placed on the PERFORM and SORT statements.

4.1 The PERFORM Statement

A PERFORM statement that appears in a section that is not in an independent segment can have within its range only one of the following:

1. Sections and/or paragraphs wholly contained in one or more non-independent segments.
2. Sections and/or paragraphs wholly contained in a single independent segment.

A PERFORM statement that appears in an independent segment can have within its range only one of the following:

1. Sections and/or paragraphs wholly contained in one or more non-independent segments.
2. Sections and/or paragraphs wholly contained in the same independent segment as that PERFORM statement.

4.2 The SORT Statement

If a SORT statement appears in a section that is not an independent segment, then any input procedures or output procedures referenced by that SORT statement must appear:

1. Totally within non-independent segments, or
2. Wholly contained in a single independent segment.

If a SORT statement appears in an independent segment, then any input procedures or output procedures referenced by that SORT statement must be contained:

1. Totally within non-independent segments, or

2. Wholly within the same independent segment as that SORT statement.

SECTION IX

Library Module

1

INTRODUCTION TO THE LIBRARY MODULE

1.1 Function

The Library module provides a capability for specifying text that is to be copied from a library.

COBOL libraries contain library texts that are available to the compiler for copying at compile time. The effect of the interpretation of the COPY statement is to insert text into the source program, where it will be treated by the compiler as part of the source program.

COBOL library text is placed on the COBOL library as a function independent of the COBOL program and according to implementor-defined techniques.

2

THE COPY STATEMENT

2.1 Function

The COPY statement incorporates text into a COBOL source program.

2.2 General Format

COPY text-name

2.3 Syntax Rules

(1)   Within one COBOL library, each text-name must be unique.

(2)   The COPY statement must be preceded by a space and terminated by the separator period.

(3)   A COPY statement may occur in the source program anywhere a character-string or a separator may occur except that a COPY statement must not occur within a COPY statement.

2.4 General Rules

(1)   The compilation of a source program containing COPY statements is logically equivalent to processing all COPY statements prior to the processing of the resulting source program.

(2)   The effect of processing a COPY statement is that the library text associated with text-name is copied into the source program, logically replacing the entire COPY statement, beginning with the

reserved word COPY and ending with the punctuation character period, inclusive.

(3)   The library text is copied unchanged.

(4)   Comment lines appearing in library text are copied into the source program unchanged.

(5)   Debugging lines are permitted within library text. If a COPY statement is specified on a debugging line, then the text that is the result of the processing of the COPY statement will appear as though it were specified on debugging lines with the following exception: comment lines in library text will appear as comment lines in the resultant source program.

(6)   The text produced as a result of the complete processing of a COPY statement must not contain a COPY statement.

(7)   The syntactic correctness of the library text cannot be independently determined. The syntactic correctness of the entire COBOL source program cannot be determined until all COPY statements have been completely processed.

(8)   Library text must conform to the rules for COBOL reference format.

SECTION X

Debug Module

1

INTRODUCTION TO THE DEBUG MODULE

1.1 Function

The Debug module in American National Standard Minimum COBOL provides a means by which the user can specify optionally compiled debugging statements.

1.2 Language Concepts

The features of the COBOL language that support the Debug module are:

1. A compile time switch—WITH DEBUGGING MODE.
2. Debugging lines.

1.2.1 A COMPILE TIME SWITCH

The WITH DEBUGGING MODE clause is written as part of the SOURCE-COMPUTER paragraph. It serves as a compile time switch over the debugging statements written in the program.

When the WITH DEBUGGING MODE clause is specified in a program, all debugging lines are compiled as specified in this section of the document. When the WITH DEBUGGING MODE clause is not specified, all debugging lines are compiled as if they were comment lines.

2

ENVIRONMENT DIVISION IN THE DEBUG MODULE

2.1 The WITH DEBUGGING MODE Clause

2.1.1 FUNCTION

The WITH DEBUGGING MODE clause indicates that all debugging lines are to be compiled. If this clause is not specified, all debugging lines are compiled as if they were comment lines.

2.1.2 GENERAL FORMAT

SOURCE-COMPUTER. computer-name [WITH DEBUG-GING MODE].

2.1.3 GENERAL RULES

(1) If the WITH DEBUGGING MODE clause is specified in the SOURCE-COMPUTER paragraph of the Configuration Section of a program, all debugging lines are compiled.

(2) If the WITH DEBUGGING MODE clause is not specified in the SOURCE-COMPUTER paragraph of the Configuration Section of a program, any debugging lines are compiled as if they were comment lines.

3

PROCEDURE DIVISION IN THE DEBUG MODULE

3.1 Debugging Lines

A debugging line is any line with a 'D' in the indicator area of the line. Any debugging line that consists solely of spaces from margin A to margin R is considered the same as a blank line.

The contents of a debugging line must be such that a syntactically correct program is formed with or without the debugging lines being considered as comment lines.

A debugging line will be considered to have all the characteristics of a comment line, if the WITH DEBUGGING MODE clause is not specified in the SOURCE-COMPUTER paragraph.

Successive debugging lines are allowed. Continuation of debugging lines is permitted, except that each continuation line must contain a 'D' in the indicator area, and character-strings may not be broken across two lines.

A debugging line is only permitted in the program after the OBJECT-COMPUTER paragraph.

Inter-Program
Communication Module

1

INTRODUCTION TO THE INTER-PROGRAM COMMUNICATION MODULE

1.1 Function

The Inter-Program Communication module provides a facility by which a program can communicate with one or more programs. This communication is provided by (1) the ability to transfer control from one program to another within a run unit and (b) the ability for both programs to have access to the same data items.

2

DATA DIVISION IN THE INTER-PROGRAM COMMUNICATION MODULE

2.1 Linkage Section

The Linkage Section in a program is meaningful if and only if the object program is to function under the control of a CALL statement, and the CALL statement in the calling program contains a USING phrase.

The Linkage Section is used for describing data that is available through the calling program but is to be referred to in both the calling and the called program. No space is allocated in the program for data items referenced by data-names in the Linkage Section of that program. Procedure Division references to these data items are resolved at object time by equating the reference in the called program to the location used in the calling program.

Data items defined in the Linkage Section of the called program may be referenced within the Procedure Division of the called program only if they are specified as operands of the USING phrase of the Procedure Division header or are subordinate to such operands, and the object program is under the control of a CALL statement that specifies a USING phrase.

The structure of the Linkage Section is the same as that previously described for the Working-Storage Section, beginning with a section header, followed by data description entries for noncontiguous data items and/or record description entries.

Each Linkage Section record-name and noncontiguous item name must be unique within the called program since it cannot be qualified.

Of those items defined in the Linkage Section only data-name-1, data-name-2, . . . in the USING phrase of the Procedure Division header and data items subordinate to these data-names may be referenced in the Procedure Division.

2.1.1 LINKAGE RECORDS

Data elements in the Linkage Section which bear a definite hierarchic relationship to one another must be grouped into records according to the rules for formation of record descriptions. Any clause which is used in an input or output record description can be used in a Linkage Section.

2.1.2 INITIAL VALUES

The VALUE clause must not be specified in the Linkage Section.

3

PROCEDURE DIVISION IN THE INTER-PROGRAM COMMUNICATION MODULE

3.1 The Procedure Division Header

The Procedure Division is identified by and must begin with the following header:

PROCEDURE DIVISION [USING data-name-1 [, data-name-2] . . .].

The USING phrase is present if and only if the object program is to function under the control of a CALL statement, and the CALL statement in the calling program contains a USING phrase.

At least five data-names must be permitted in the USING phrase of the Procedure Division header.

Each of the operands in the USING phrase of the Procedure Division header must be defined as a data item in the Linkage Section of the program in which this header occurs, and it must have a 01 level-number.

Within a called program, Linkage Section data items are processed according to their data descriptions given in the called program.

When the USING phrase is present, the object program operates as if data-name-1 of the Procedure Division header in the called program and data-name-1 in the USING phrase of the CALL statement in the calling program refer to a single set of data that is equally available to both the called and calling programs. Their descriptions must define an equal number of character positions; however, they need not be the same name. In like manner, there is an equivalent relationship between data-name-2, . . ., in the USING phrase of the called program and data-name-2, . . ., in the USING phrase of the CALL statement in the calling program. A data-name must not appear more than once in the USING phrase in the Procedure Division header of the called program; however, a given data-name may appear more than once in the same USING phrase of a CALL statement.

3.2 The CALL Statement

3.2.1 FUNCTION

The CALL statement causes control to be transferred from one object program to another, within the run unit.

3.2.2 GENERAL FORMAT

CALL literal [USING data-name-1 [, data-name-2] . . .]

3.2.3 SYNTAX RULES

(1)   Literal must be a nonnumeric literal.

(2)   The USING phrase is included in the CALL statement only if there is a USING phrase in the Procedure Division header of the called program and the number of operands in each USING phrase must be identical.

(3)   At least five data-names must be permitted in the USING phrase of the CALL statement.

(4)   Each of the operands in the USING phrase must have been defined as a data item in the File Section, Working-Storage Section, Communication Section, or Linkage Section, and must have a level-number of 01.

3.2.4 GENERAL RULES

(1)   The program whose name is specified by the value of literal is the called program; the program in which the CALL statement appears is the calling program.

(2)   The execution of a CALL statement causes control to pass to the called program.

(3)   A called program is in its initial state the first time it is called within a run unit.

On all other entries into the called program, the state of the program remains unchanged from its state when last exited. This includes all data fields and the status and positioning of all files.

(4)   If during the execution of the CALL statement, it is determined that the available portion of object time memory is incapable of accommodating the program specified in the CALL statement, the effects of the CALL statement are defined by the implementor.

(5)   Called programs may contain CALL statements. However, a called program must not contain a CALL statement that directly or indirectly calls the calling program.

(6)   The data-names, specified by the USING phrase of the CALL statement, indicate those data items available to a calling program that may be referred to in the called program. The order of appearance of the data-names in the USING phrase of the CALL statement and the USING phrase in the Procedure Division header is critical. Corresponding data-names refer to a single set of data which is available to the called and calling program. The correspondence is positional, not by name.

(7)   The CALL statement may appear anywhere within a segmented program. The implementor must provide all controls necessary to insure that the proper logic flow is maintained. Therefore, when a CALL statement appears in a section with a segment-number greater than or equal to 50, that segment is in its last used state when the EXIT PROGRAM statement returns control to the calling program.

3.3 The EXIT PROGRAM Statement

3.3.1 FUNCTION

The EXIT PROGRAM statement marks the logical end of a called program.

3.3.2 GENERAL FORMAT

EXIT PROGRAM.

3.3.3 SYNTAX RULES

(1) The EXIT PROGRAM statement must appear in a sentence by itself.

(2) The EXIT PROGRAM sentence must be the only sentence in the paragraph.

3.3.4 GENERAL RULES

(1) An execution of an EXIT PROGRAM statement in a called program causes control to be passed to the calling program. If the EXIT PROGRAM statement is executed in a program which is not under the control of a calling program, the EXIT PROGRAM statement causes execution of the program to continue with the next executable statement.

SECTION XII

Communication Module

1

INTRODUCTION TO THE COMMUNICATION MODULE

1.1 Function

The Communication module provides the ability to access, process, and create messages. It provides the ability to communicate through a Message Control System with local and remote communication devices.

2

DATA DIVISION IN THE COMMUNICATION MODULE

2.1 Communication Section

In a ĊOBOL program the communication description entries (CD) represent the highest level of organization in the Communication Section. The Communication Section header is followed by a communication description entry consisting of a level indicator (CD), a data-name and a series of independent clauses. These clauses indicate the queues and sub-queues, the message date and time, the source, the text length, the status and end keys, and message count of input. These clauses specify the destination count, the text length, the status and error keys, and destinations for output. The entry itself is terminated by a period.

2.2 The Communication Description—Complete Entry Skeleton

2.2.1 FUNCTION

The communication description specifies the interface area between the MCS and a COBOL program.

2.2.2 GENERAL FORMAT

Format 1

CD cd-name; FOR INPUT

    [; SYMBOLIC QUEUE IS data-name-1]

    [; MESSAGE DATE IS data-name-2]

    [; MESSAGE TIME IS data-name-3]

    [; SYMBOLIC SOURCE IS data-name-4]

[; TEXT LENGTH IS data-name-5]
[; END KEY IS data-name-6]
[; STATUS KEY is data-name-7]
[; MESSAGE COUNT IS data-name-8].

Format 2
CD cd-name; FOR OUTPUT
    [; DESTINATION COUNT IS data-name-1]
    [; TEXT LENGTH IS data-name-2]
    [; STATUS KEY IS data-name-3]
    [; ERROR KEY IS data-name-4]
    [; SYMBOLIC DESTINATION IS data-name-5].

2.2.3 SYNTAX RULES

Format 1:

(1) A CD must appear only in the Communication Section

(2) The optional clauses may be written in any order.

(3) For each input CD, a record area of 87 contiguous standard data format characters is allocated. This record area is defined to the MCS as follows:

(a) The SYMBOLIC QUEUE clause defines data-name-1 as the name of an elementary alphanumeric data item of 12 characters occupying positions 1–12 in the record.

(b) Positions 13–48 in the record are reserved compatibility with X3.23–1974.

(c) The MESSAGE DATE clause defines data-name-2 as the name of a data item whose implicit description is that of an integer of 6 digits without an operational sign occupying character positions 49–54 in the record.

(d) The MESSAGE TIME clause defines data-name-3 as the name of a data item whose implicit description is that of an integer of 8 digits without an operational sign occupying character positions 55–62 in the record.

(e) The SYMBOLIC SOURCE clause defines data-name-4 as the name of an elementary alphanumeric data item of 12 characters occupying positions 63–74 in the record.

(f) The TEXT LENGTH clause defines data-name-5 as the name of an elementary data item whose implicit description is that of an integer of 4 digits without an optional sign occupying character positions 75–78 in the record.

(g) The END KEY clause defines data-name-6 as the name of an elementary alphanumeric data item of 1 character occupying position 79 in the record.

(h) The STATUS KEY clause defines data-name-7 as the name of an elementary alphanumeric data item of 2 characters occupying positions 80–81 in the record.

(i) The MESSAGE COUNT clause defines data-name-8 as the name of an elementary data item whose implicit description is that of an integer of 6 digits without an operational sign occupying character positions 82–87 in the record.

The communication description results in a record whose implicit description is equivalent to the following:

Implicit Description	Comment
01 data-name-0.	
02 data-name-1 PICTURE X (12).	SYMBOLIC QUEUE
02 FILLER PICTURE X (36).	
02 data-name-2 PICTURE X (6).	MESSAGE DATE
02 data-name-3 PICTURE 9 (8).	MESSAGE TIME
02 data-name-4 PICTURE X (12).	SYMBOLIC SOURCE
02 data-name-5 PICTURE 9 (4).	TEXT LENGTH
02 data-name-6 PICTURE X.	END KEY
02 data-name-7 PICTURE XX.	STATUS KEY
02 data-name-8 PICTURE 9 (6).	MESSAGE COUNT

NOTE: In the above, the information under 'Comment' is for clarification and is not part of the description.

(4) Data-name-1, data-name-2, ..., data-name-8 must be unique within the CD. Within this series, any data-name may be replaced by the reserved word FILLER.

Format 2:

(5) A CD must appear only in the Communication Section.

(6) For each output CD, a record area of 23 contiguous standard data format characters is allocated.

(a) The DESTINATION COUNT clause defines data-name-1 as the name of a data item whose implicit description is that of an integer without an operational sign occupying character positions 1–4 in the record.

(b) The TEXT LENGTH clause defines data-name-2 as the name of an elementary data item whose implicit description is that of an integer of 4 digits without an operational sign occupying character positions 5–8 in the record.

(c) The STATUS KEY clause defines data-name-3 to be an elementary alphanumeric data item of 2 characters occupying positions 9–10 in the record.

(d) Character positions 11–23 will form items of the following description:

1. The ERROR KEY clause defines data-name-4 as the name of an elementary alphanumeric data item of 1 character.

2. The SYMBOLIC DESTINATION clause defines data-name-5 as the name of an elementary alphanumeric data item of 12 characters.

Use of the above clauses results in a record whose implicit description is equivalent to the following:

Implicit Description	Comment
01 data-name-0.	
02 data-name-1 PICTURE 9 (4).	DESTINATION COUNT

02 data-name-2 PICTURE 9 (4).	TEXT LENGTH
02 data-name-3 PICTURE XX.	STATUS KEY
02 data-name	DESTINATION TABLE
03 data-name-4 PICTURE X.	ERROR KEY
03 data-name-5 PICTURE X (12).	SYMBOLIC DESTINATION

NOTE: In the above, the information under 'Comment' is for clarification and is not part of the description.

(7)   Data-name-1, data-name-2, . . ., data-name-5 must be unique within a CD.

(8)   The value of the data item referenced by data-name-1 must be 1.

2.2.4 GENERAL RULES

Format 1:

(1)   The input CD information constitutes the communication between the MCS and the program as information about the message being handled. This information does not come from the terminal as part of the message.

(2)   The contents of positions 13–48 in the record must contain spaces.

(3)   The data item referenced by data-name-1 contains a symbolic name designating a queue. A symbolic name must follow the rules for the formation of system-names, and must have been previously defined to the MCS.

(4)   A RECEIVE statement causes the serial return of the 'next' message from the queue as specified by the entries in the CD. After execution of a RECEIVE statement, the content of the data item referenced by data-name-1 will contain the symbolic name of the queue.

(5) Data-name-2 has the format 'YYMMDD' (year, month, day). Its contents represent the date on which the MCS recognizes that the message is complete.

The contents of the data item referenced by data-name-2 are only updated by the MCS as part of the execution of a RECEIVE statement.

(6) The contents of data-name-3 has the format 'HHMMSSTT' (hours, minutes, seconds, hundredths of a second) and its contents represent the time at which the MCS recognizes that the message is complete.

The contents of the data item referenced by data-name-3 are only updated by the MCS as part of the execution of the RE-CEIVE statement.

(7) During the execution of a RECEIVE statement, the MCS provides, in the data item referenced by data-name-4, the symbolic name of the communications terminal that is the source of the message being transferred. However, if the symbolic name of the communication terminal is not known to the MCS, the contents of the data item referenced by data-name-4 will contain spaces.

(8) The MCS indicates via the contents of the data item referenced by data-name-5 the number of character positions filled as a result of the execution of the RECEIVE statement.

(9) The contents of the data item referenced by data-name-6 are set only by the MCS as part of the execution of a RECEIVE statement according to the following rules:

(a) When the RECEIVE MESSAGE phrase is specified, then:

1. If an end of group has been detected, the contents of the data item referenced by data-name-6 are set to 3;
2. If an end of message has been detected, the contents of the data item referenced by data-name-6 are set to 2.

(b) When more than one of the above conditions is satisfied simultaneously, the rule first satisfied in the order listed determines the contents of the data item referenced by data-name-6.

(10) The contents of the data item referenced by data-name-7 indicate the status condition of the previously executed RECEIVE, or ACCEPT MESSAGE COUNT statements.

The actual association between the contents of the data item referenced by data-name-7 and the status condition itself is defined in Table 1.

RECEIVE	END	ACCEPT MESSAGE COUNT	STATUS KEY CODE	
X	X	X	00	No error detected. Action completed.
	X		10	Destination is disabled. Action completed.
	X		20	Destination unknown. No action taken for unknown destination. Data-name-4 (ERROR KEY) indicates unknown.
X		X	20	Queues unknown. No action taken.
	X		30	Content of DESTINATION COUNT invalid. No action taken.
	X		50	Character count greater than length of sending field. No action taken.

Table 1 Communication Status Key Condition

2: Data Division in the Communication Module

(11) The contents of the data item referenced by data-name-8 indicate the number of messages that exist in a queue. The MCS updates the contents of the data item referenced by data-name-8 only as part of the execution of an ACCEPT statement with the COUNT phrase.

Format 2:

(12) The nature of the output CD information is such that it is not sent to the terminal, but constitutes the communication between the program and the MCS as information about the message being handled.

(13) During the execution of a SEND statement, the contents of the data item referenced by data-name-1 will indicate to the MCS the number of symbolic destinations that are to be used from the area referenced by data-name-5.
    The MCS finds the symbolic destination in the area referenced by data-name-5.
    If during the execution of a SEND statement, the value of the data item referenced by data-name-1 is outside the range of 1, an error condition is indicated and the execution of the SEND statement is terminated.

(14) It is the responsibility of the user to insure that the value of the data item referenced by data-name-1 is valid at the time of execution of the SEND statement.

(14) It is the responsibility of the user to insure that the value of the data item referenced by data-name-1 is valid at the time of execution of the SEND statement.

(15) As part of the execution of a SEND statement, the MCS will interpret the contents of the data item referenced by data-name-2 to be the user's indication of the number of leftmost character positions of the data item referenced by the associated SEND identifier from which data is to be transferred.

(16) The data item referenced by data-name-5 contains a symbolic destination previously known to the MCS. These symbolic

destination names must follow the rules for the formation of system-names.

(17) The contents of the data item referenced by data-name-3 indicate the status condition of the previously executed SEND statement.

The actual association between the contents of the data item referenced by data-name-3 and the status condition itself is defined in Table 1.

(18) If, during the execution of a SEND statement, the MCS determines that any specified destination is unknown, the contents of the data item referenced by data-name-3 and data-name-4 are updated.

The contents of the data item referenced by data-name-4 when equal to 1 indicate that the associated value in the area referenced by data-name-5 has not been previously defined to the MCS. Otherwise, the contents of the data item referenced by data-name-4 are set to zero (0).

<u>All Formats:</u>

(19) Table 1 indicates the possible contents of the data items referenced by data-name-7 for Format 1 and by data-name-3 for Format 2 at the completion of each statement shown. An 'X' on a line in a statement column indicates that the associated code shown for that line is possible for that statement.

3

PROCEDURE DIVISION IN THE COMMUNICATION MODULE

3.1 The ACCEPT MESSAGE COUNT Statement

3.1.1 FUNCTION

The ACCEPT MESSAGE COUNT statement causes the number of messages in a queue to be made available.

3.1.2 GENERAL FORMAT

ACCEPT cd-name MESSAGE COUNT

3.1.3 SYNTAX RULES

(1)   Cd-name must reference an input CD.

3.1.4 GENERAL RULES

(1)   The ACCEPT MESSAGE COUNT statement causes the MESSAGE COUNT field specified for cd-name to be updated to indicate the number of messages that exist in a queue.

(2)   Upon execution of the ACCEPT MESSAGE COUNT statement, the contents of the area specified by a communication description entry must contain at least the name of the symbolic queue to be tested. Testing the condition causes the contents of the data items referenced by data-name-7 (STATUS KEY) and data-name-8 (MESSAGE COUNT) of the area associated with the communication entry to be appropriately updated. (See The Communication Description—Complete Entry Skeleton.)

3.2 The RECEIVE Statement

3.2.1 FUNCTION

The RECEIVE statement makes available to the COBOL program a message, and pertinent information about the data from a queue maintained by the Message Control System. The RECEIVE statement allows for a specific imperative statement when no data is available.

3.2.2 GENERAL FORMAT

RECEIVE cd-name MESSAGE INTO identifier-1 [; NO DATA imperative-statement]

3.2.3 SYNTAX RULES

(1) Cd-name must reference an input CD.

3.2.4 GENERAL RULES

(1) The contents of the data item specified by data-name-1 (SYMBOLIC QUEUE) of the area referenced by cd-name designates the queue structure containing the message. (See The CD Entry.)

(2) The message is transferred to the receiving character positions of the area referenced by identifier-1 aligned to the left without space fill.

(3) When during the execution of a RECEIVE statement, the MCS makes data available in the data item referenced by identifier-1, control is transferred to the next executable statement, whether or not the NO DATA phrase is specified.

(4) When, during the execution of a RECEIVE statement, the MCS does not make data available in the data item referenced by identifier-1:

(a) If the NO DATA phrase is specified, the RECEIVE operation is terminated with the indication that action is

310

complete (see general rule 5), and the imperative statement in the NO DATA phrase is executed.

(b) If the NO DATA phrase is not specified, execution of the object program is suspended until data is made available in the data item referenced by identifier-1.

(c) If one or more queues is unknown to the MCS, control passes to the next executable statement, whether or not the NO DATA phrase is specified. (See Communication Status Key Condition.)

(5) The data item identified by the input CD are appropriately updated by the Message Control System at each execution of a RECEIVE statement. (See The CD Entry.)

(6) A single execution of a RECEIVE statement never returns to the data item referenced by identifier-1 more than a single message.

(7) End of segment indicators are ignored, and the following rules apply to the data transfer:

(a) If a message is the same size as the area referenced by identifier-1, the message is stored in the area referenced by identifier-1.

(b) If a message size is less than the area referenced by identifier-1, the message is aligned to the leftmost character position of the area referenced by identifier-1 with no space file.

(c) If a message size is greater than the area referenced by identifier-1, the message fills the area referenced by identifier-1 left to right starting with the leftmost character of the message. The disposition of the remainder of the message is undefined.

(8) After the execution of a STOP RUN statement, the disposition of a remaining portion of a message partially obtained in that run unit is defined by the implementor. (See page 163, The STOP Statement.)

3.3 The SEND Statement

3.3.1 FUNCTION

The SEND statement causes a message to be released to one output queue maintained by the Message Control System.

3.3.2 GENERAL FORMAT

SEND cd-name

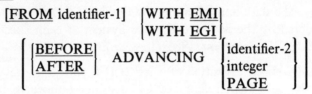

3.3.3 SYNTAX RULES

(1) Cd-name must reference an output CD.

(2) Integer may be zero.

3.3.4 GENERAL RULES

(1) When a receiving communication device (printer, display screen, card punch, etc.) is oriented to a fixed line size:

(a). Each message will begin at the leftmost character position of the physical line.

(b) A message that is smaller than the physical line size is released so as to appear space-filled to the right.

(c) Excess characters of a message will not be truncated. Characters will be placed to a size equal to that of the physical line and then outputted to the device. The process continues on the next line with the excess characters.

(2) When a receiving communication device (paper tape punch, another computer, etc.) is oriented to handle variable length mes-

sages, each message will begin on the next available character position of the communications device.

(3)   As part of the execution of a SEND statement, the MCS will interpret the contents of the data item referenced by data-name-2 (TEXT LENGTH) of the area referenced by cd-name to be the user's indication of the number of leftmost character positions of the data item referenced by identifier-1 from which data is to be transferred.

If the contents of the data item referenced by data-name-2 (TEXT LENGTH) of the area referenced by cd-name are zero, no characters of the data item referenced by identifier-1 are transferred.

If the contents of the data item referenced by data-name-2 (TEXT LENGTH) of the area referenced by cd-name are outside the range of zero through the size of the data item referenced by identifier-1 inclusive, an error is indicated by the value of the data item referenced by data-name-3 (STATUS KEY) of the area referenced by cd-name, and no data is transferred. (See Communication Status Key Condition.)

(4)   As part of the execution of a SEND statement, the contents of the data item referenced by data-name-3 (STATUS KEY) of the area referenced by cd-name is updated by the MCS. (See The CD Entry.)

(5)   The effect of having special control characters within the contents of the data item referenced by identifier-1 is undefined.

(6)   A single execution of a SEND statement releases to the MCS a single message as indicated by the specified indicator EMI or EGI.

(7)   The EMI indicates to the MCS that the message is complete. The EGI indicates to the MCS that the group of messages is complete. The implementor will specify the interpretation that is given to the EGI by the MCS.

The MCS will recognize these indications and establish whatever is necessary to maintain group and message control.

(8) The hierarchy of ending indicators is EGI and EMI. An EGI need not be preceded by an EMI.

(9) The ADVANCING phrase allows control of the vertical positioning of each message or on a communication device where vertical positioning is applicable. If vertical positioning is not applicable on the device, the MCS will ignore the vertical positioning specified or implied.

(10) On a device where vertical positioning is applicable and the ADVANCING phrase is not specified, automatic advancing will be provided by the implementor to act as if the user had specified AFTER ADVANCING 1.

(11) If the ADVANCING phrase is implicitly or explicitly specified and vertical positioning is applicable, the following rules apply:

(a) If identifier-2 or integer is specified, characters transmitted to the communication device will be repositioned vertically downward the number of lines equal to the value associated with the data item referenced by identifier-2 or integer.

(b) If the BEFORE phrase is used, the message is represented on the communication device before vertical repositioning according to general rule 11a above.

(c) If the AFTER phrase is used, the message is represented on the communication device after vertical repositioning according to general rule 11a above.

(d) If PAGE is specified, characters transmitted to the communication device will be represented on the device before or after (depending upon the phrase used) the device is repositioned to the next page. If PAGE is specified but page has no meaning in conjunction with a specific device, then advancing will be provided by the implementor to act as if the user had specified BEFORE or AFTER (depending upon the phrase used) ADVANCING 1.

INDEX